CLEP College Mathematics Practice Workbook

2022

The Most Comprehensive Review for the CLEP College Mathematics Test

By

Reza Nazari

All inquiries should be addressed to:
info@effortlessMath.com
www.EffortlessMath.com

ISBN: 978-1-63719-051-7

Published by: **Effortless Math Education Inc.**

For Online Math Practice Visit www.EffortlessMath.com

Welcome to
CLEP College Mathematics Prep 2022

Thank you for choosing Effortless Math for your CLEP College Mathematics test preparation and congratulations on making the decision to take the CLEP College Mathematics test! It's a remarkable move you are taking, one that shouldn't be diminished in any capacity.

That's why you need to use every tool possible to ensure you succeed on the test with the highest possible score, and this extensive math workbook is one such tool.

If math has never been a strong subject for you, don't worry! This book along with our online CLEP College Mathematics resources will help you prepare for (and even ACE) the CLEP College Mathematics test. As test day draws nearer, effective preparation becomes increasingly more important. Thankfully, you have this comprehensive workbook to help you get ready for the test. With this book and Effortless Math online resources, you can feel confident that you will be more than ready for the CLEP College Mathematics test when the time comes.

First and foremost, it is important to note that this book is a workbook and not a textbook. Every lesson of this practice book was carefully developed to ensure that you are making the most effective use of your time while preparing for the test. This up-to-date book reflects the 2022 test guidelines and will put you on the right track to hone your math skills, overcome exam anxiety, and boost your confidence, so that you can have your best to succeed on the CLEP College Mathematics test.

This exercise book will:

☑ Explain the format of the CLEP College Mathematics test.

☑ Describe specific test-taking strategies that you can use on the test.

☑ Provide CLEP College Mathematics test-taking tips.

☑ Help you identify the areas in which you need to concentrate your study time.

☑ Offer exercises that help you develop the basic math skills you will learn in each section.

☑ Give **2 realistic and full-length practice tests** (featuring new question types) with detailed answers to help you measure your exam readiness and build confidence.

This resource contains comprehensive practice questions and exercises that you will need to prepare for the CLEP College Mathematics test. You'll get numerous skill building exercises as well as tips and techniques on how to prepare for your CLEP College Mathematics test.

In addition, in the following pages you'll find:

➢ **How to Use This Book Effectively** – This section provides you with step-by-step instructions on how to get the most out of this comprehensive study guide.

➢ **How to study for the CLEP College Mathematics Test** – A six-step study program has been developed to help you make the best use of this book and prepare for your CLEP College Mathematics test. Here you'll find tips and strategies to guide your study program and help you understand CLEP College Mathematics and how to ace the test.

➤ **CLEP College Mathematics Review** – Learn everything you need to know about the CLEP College Mathematics test.

➤ **CLEP College Mathematics Test-Taking Strategies** – Learn how to effectively put these recommended test-taking techniques into use for improving your CLEP College Mathematics score.

➤ **Test Day Tips** – Review these tips to make sure you will do your best when the big day comes.

Effortless Math's CLEP College Mathematics Online Center

Effortless Math Online CLEP College Mathematics Center offers a complete study program, including the following:

✓ Step-by-step instructions on how to prepare for the CLEP College Mathematics test

✓ Numerous CLEP College Mathematics worksheets to help you measure your math skills

✓ Complete list of CLEP College Mathematics formulas

✓ Video lessons for all CLEP College Mathematics topics

✓ Full-length CLEP College Mathematics practice tests

✓ And much more…

No Registration Required.

Visit **EffortlessMath.com/CLEP** to find your online CLEP College Mathematics resources.

How to Use This Book Effectively

L ook no further when you need a study program to improve your math skills to succeed on the math portion of the CLEP College Mathematics test. Each chapter of this comprehensive workbook will provide you with the knowledge, tools, and understanding needed for every topic covered on the test.

It's imperative that you understand each topic before moving onto another one, as that's the way to guarantee your success. You can use Effortless Math online course (a free course) to find examples and a step-by-step guide of every math concept in this workbook to better understand the content that will be on the test. To get the best possible results from this book:

➢ **Begin studying long before your test date**. This provides you ample time to learn the different math concepts. The earlier you begin studying for the test, the sharper your skills will be. Do not procrastinate! Provide yourself with plenty of time to learn the concepts and feel comfortable that you understand them when your test date arrives.

➢ **Practice consistently**. Study CLEP College Mathematics concepts at least 20 to 30 minutes a day. Remember, slow and steady wins the race, which can be applied to preparing for the CLEP College Mathematics test. Instead of cramming to tackle everything at once, be patient and learn the math topics in short bursts.

➢ Whenever you get a math problem wrong, **mark it off, and review it later** to make sure you understand the concept.

➢ Start each session by **looking over the previous material.**

➢ Once you've reviewed the book's exercises, **take a practice test at the back of the book** to gauge your level of readiness. Then, review your results. Read detailed answers and solutions for each question you missed.

➢ **Take another practice test** to get an idea of how ready you are to take the actual exam. Taking the practice tests will give you the confidence you need on test day. Simulate the CLEP College Mathematics testing environment by sitting in a quiet room free from distraction. Make sure to clock yourself with a timer.

How to Study for the CLEP College Mathematics Test

Studying for the CLEP College Mathematics test can be a really daunting and boring task. What's the best way to go about it? Is there a certain study method that works better than others? Well, studying for the CLEP College Mathematics can be done effectively. The following six-step program has been designed to make preparing for the CLEP College Mathematics test more efficient and less overwhelming.

Step **1** - Create a study plan
Step **2** - Choose your study resources
Step **3** - Review, Learn, Practice
Step **4** - Learn and practice test-taking strategies
Step **5** - Learn the CLEP College Mathematics Test format and take practice tests
Step **6** - Analyze your performance

STEP 1: Create a Study Plan

It's always easier to get things done when you have a plan. Creating a study plan for the CLEP College Mathematics test can help you to stay on track with your studies. It's important to sit down and prepare a study plan with what works with your life, work, and any other obligations you may have. Devote enough time each day to studying. It's also a

great idea to break down each section of the exam into blocks and study one concept at a time.

It's important to understand that there is no "right" way to create a study plan. Your study plan will be personalized based on your specific needs and learning style.

Follow these guidelines to create an effective study plan for your CLEP College Mathematics test:

★ **Analyze your learning style and study habits** – Everyone has a different learning style. It is essential to embrace your individuality and the unique way you learn. Think about what works and what doesn't work for you. Do you prefer CLEP College Mathematics prep books or a combination of textbooks and video lessons? Does it work better for you if you study every night for thirty minutes or is it more effective to study in the morning before going to work?

★ **Evaluate your schedule** – Review your current schedule and find out how much time you can consistently devote to CLEP College Mathematics study.

★ **Develop a schedule** – Now it's time to add your study schedule to your calendar like any other obligation. Schedule time for study, practice, and review. Plan out which topic you will study on which day to ensure that you're devoting enough time to each concept. Develop a study plan that is mindful, realistic, and flexible.

★ **Stick to your schedule** – A study plan is only effective when it is followed consistently. You should try to develop a study plan that you can follow for the length of your study program.

★ **Evaluate your study plan and adjust as needed** – Sometimes you need to adjust your plan when you have new commitments. Check in with yourself regularly to make sure that you're not falling behind in your study plan. Remember, the most important thing is sticking to your plan. Your study plan is all about helping you be more productive. If you find that your study plan is not as effective as you want, don't get discouraged. It's okay to make changes as you figure out what works best for you.

STEP 2: Choose Your Study Resources

There are numerous textbooks and online resources available for the CLEP College Mathematics test, and it may not be clear where to begin. Don't worry! This exercise book reviews all CLEP College Mathematics concepts and topics. In addition to the book content, you can also use Effortless Math's online resources. (video lessons, worksheets,

formulas, etc.) On each page, there is a link (and a QR code) to an online webpage which provides a comprehensive review of the topic, step-by-step instruction, video tutorial, and numerous examples and exercises to help you fully understand the concept.

Simply visit EffortlessMath.com/CLEP to find your online CLEP College Mathematics resources.

STEP 3: Review, Learn, Practice

This CLEP College Mathematics exercise book breaks down each subject into specific skills or content areas. For instance, the percent concept is separated into different topics—percent calculation, percent increase and decrease, percent problems, etc. Use this book to help you go over all key math concepts and topics on the CLEP College Mathematics test.

As you review each topic, take notes or highlight the concepts you would like to go over again in the future. If you're unfamiliar with a topic or something is difficult for you, use the link (or the **QR** code) at the top of the page to find the webpage that provides more instruction about that topic. For each math topic, plenty of instructions, step-by-step guides, and examples are provided to ensure you get a good grasp of the material.

Quickly review the topics you do understand to get a brush-up of the material. Be sure to do the practice questions provided at the end of every chapter to measure your understanding of the concepts.

STEP 4: Learn and Practice Test-taking Strategies

In the following sections, you will find important test-taking strategies and tips that can help you earn extra points. You'll learn how to think strategically and when to guess if you don't know the answer to a question. Using CLEP College Mathematics test-taking strategies and tips can help you raise your score and do well on the test. Apply test taking strategies on the practice tests to help you boost your confidence.

STEP 5: Learn the CLEP College Mathematics Test Format and Take Practice Tests

The CLEP College Mathematics *Test Review* section provides information about the structure of the CLEP College Mathematics test. Read this section to learn more about the CLEP College Mathematics test structure, different test sections, the number of questions in each section, and the section time limits. When you have a prior understanding of the test format and different types of CLEP College Mathematics questions, you'll feel more confident when you take the actual exam.

Once you have read through the instructions and lessons and feel like you are ready to go – take advantage of both of the full-length CLEP College Mathematics practice tests available in this exercise book. Use the practice tests to sharpen your skills and build confidence.

The CLEP College Mathematics practice tests offered at the end of the book are formatted similarly to the actual CLEP College Mathematics test. When you take each practice test, try to simulate actual testing conditions. To take the practice tests, sit in a quiet space, time yourself, and work through as many of the questions as time allows. The practice tests are followed by detailed answer explanations to help you find your weak areas, learn from your mistakes, and raise your CLEP College Mathematics score.

STEP 6: Analyze Your Performance

After taking the practice tests, look over the answer keys and explanations to learn which questions you answered correctly and which you did not. Never be discouraged if you make a few mistakes. See them as a learning opportunity. This will highlight your strengths and weaknesses.

You can use the results to determine if you need additional practice or if you are ready to take the actual CLEP College Mathematics test.

Looking for more?

Visit <u>EffortlessMath.com/CLEP</u> to find hundreds of CLEP College Mathematics worksheets, video tutorials, practice tests, CLEP College Mathematics formulas, and much more.

Or scan this QR code.

No Registration Required.

CLEP College Mathematics Test Review

College -Level Examination Program (CLEP) is a series of 33 standardized tests that measures your knowledge of certain subjects. You can earn college credit at thousands of colleges and universities by earning a satisfactory score on a computer based CLEP exam.

The CLEP College Mathematics measures your knowledge of math topics generally taught in a college course for non-mathematics majors. It contains approximately 60 multiple choice questions to be answered in 90 minutes. Some of these questions are pretest questions that will not be scored. These 60 questions cover: sets, logic, the real number system, functions and graphing, probability and statistics, and additional topics from algebra and geometry. A scientific calculator is available to students during the entire testing time. The CLEP College mathematics exam score ranges from 20 to 80 converting to A, B, C, or D based on this score. The letter grade is applied to your college course equivalent.

CLEP College Mathematics Test-Taking Strategies

Here are some test-taking strategies that you can use to maximize your performance and results on the CLEP College Mathematics test.

#1: Use This Approach To Answer Every CLEP College Mathematics Question

- Review the question to identify keywords and important information.
- Translate the keywords into math operations so you can solve the problem.
- Review the answer choices. What are the differences between answer choices?
- Draw or label a diagram if needed.
- Try to find patterns.
- Find the right method to answer the question. Use straightforward math, plug in numbers, or test the answer choices (backsolving).
- Double-check your work.

#2: Use Educated Guessing

This approach is applicable to the problems you understand to some degree but cannot solve using straightforward math. In such cases, try to filter out as many answer choices as possible before picking an answer. In cases where you don't have a clue about what a certain problem entails, don't waste any time trying to eliminate answer choices. Just choose one randomly before moving onto the next question.

As you can ascertain, direct solutions are the most optimal approach. Carefully read through the question, determine what the solution is using the math you have learned before, then coordinate the answer with one of the choices available to you. Are you stumped? Make your best guess, then move on.

Don't leave any fields empty! Even if you're unable to work out a problem, strive to answer it. Take a guess if you have to. You will not lose points by getting an answer wrong, though you may gain a point by getting it correct!

#3 : BALLPARK

A ballpark answer is a rough approximation. When we become overwhelmed by calculations and figures, we end up making silly mistakes. A decimal that is moved by one unit can change an answer from right to wrong, regardless of the number of steps that you went through to get it. That's where ballparking can play a big part.

If you think you know what the correct answer may be (even if it's just a ballpark answer), you'll usually have the ability to eliminate a couple of choices. While answer choices are usually based on the average student error and/or values that are closely tied, you will still be able to weed out choices that are way far afield. Try to find answers that aren't in the proverbial ballpark when you're looking for a wrong answer on a multiple-choice question. This is an optimal approach to eliminating answers to a problem.

#4 : BACKSOLVING

All questions on the CLEP College Mathematics test will be in multiple-choice format. Many test-takers prefer multiple-choice questions, as at least the answer is right there. You'll typically have four answers to pick from. You simply need to figure out which one is correct. Usually, the best way to go about doing so is "backsolving."

As mentioned earlier, direct solutions are the most optimal approach to answering a question. Carefully read through a problem, calculate a solution, then correspond the answer with one of the choices displayed in front of you. If you can't calculate a solution, your next best approach involves "backsolving."

When backsolving a problem, contrast one of your answer options against the problem you are asked, then see which of them is most relevant. More often than not, answer choices are listed in ascending or descending order. In such cases, try out the choices B or C. If it's not correct, you can go either down or up from there.

#5 : PLUGGING IN NUMBERS

"Plugging in numbers" is a strategy that can be applied to a wide range of different math problems on the CLEP College Mathematics test. This approach is typically used to simplify a challenging question so that it is more understandable. By using the strategy carefully, you can find the answer without too much trouble.

The concept is fairly straightforward—replace unknown variables in a problem with certain values. When selecting a number, consider the following:

- Choose a number that's basic (just not too basic). Generally, you should avoid choosing 1 (or even 0). A decent choice is 2.

- Try not to choose a number that is displayed in the problem.

- Make sure you keep your numbers different if you need to choose at least two of them.

- More often than not, choosing numbers merely lets you filter out some of your answer choices. As such, don't just go with the first choice that gives you the right answer.

- If several answers seem correct, then you'll need to choose another value and try again. This time, though, you'll just need to check choices that haven't been eliminated yet.

- If your question contains fractions, then a potential right answer may involve either an LCD (least common denominator) or an LCD multiple.

- 100 is the number you should choose when you are dealing with problems involving percentages.

CLEP College Mathematics – Test Day Tips

After practicing and reviewing all the math concepts you've been taught, and taking some CLEP College Mathematics practice tests, you'll be prepared for test day. Consider the following tips to be extra-ready come test time.

Before Your Test

What to do the night before:

- **Relax!** One day before your test, study lightly or skip studying altogether. You shouldn't attempt to learn something new, either. There are plenty of reasons why studying the evening before a big test can work against you. Put it this way–a marathoner wouldn't go out for a sprint before the day of a big race. Mental marathoners–such as yourself–should not study for any more than one hour 24 hours before a CLEP College Mathematics test. That's because your brain requires some rest to be at its best. The night before your exam, spend some time with family or friends, or read a book.

- **Avoid bright screens** - You'll have to get some good shuteye the night before your test. Bright screens (such as the ones coming from your laptop, TV, or mobile device) should be avoided altogether. Staring at such a screen will keep your brain up, making it hard to drift asleep at a reasonable hour.

- **Make sure your dinner is healthy** - The meal that you have for dinner should be nutritious. Be sure to drink plenty of water as well. Load up on your complex carbohydrates, much like a marathon runner would do. Pasta, rice, and potatoes are ideal options here, as are vegetables and protein sources.

- **Get your bag ready for test day** - The night prior to your test, pack your bag with your stationery, admissions pass, ID, and any other gear that you need. Keep the bag right by your front door.

- **Make plans to reach the testing site** - Before going to sleep, ensure that you understand precisely how you will arrive at the site of the test. If parking is something you'll have to find first, plan for it. If you're dependent on public transit, then review the schedule. You should also make sure that the train/bus/subway/streetcar you use will be running. Find out about road closures as well. If a parent or friend is accompanying you, ensure that they understand what steps they have to take as well.

The Day of the Test

- **Get up reasonably early, but not too early.**

- **Have breakfast** - Breakfast improves your concentration, memory, and mood. As such, make sure the breakfast that you eat in the morning is healthy. The last thing you want to be is distracted by a grumbling tummy. If it's not your own stomach making those noises, another test taker close to you might be instead. Prevent discomfort or embarrassment by consuming a healthy breakfast. Bring a snack with you if you think you'll need it.

- **Follow your daily routine** - Do you watch Good Morning America each morning while getting ready for the day? Don't break your usual habits on the day of the test. Likewise, if coffee isn't something you drink in the morning, then don't take up the habit hours before your test. Routine consistency lets you concentrate on the main objective—doing the best you can on your test.

- **Wear layers** - Dress yourself up in comfortable layers. You should be ready for any kind of internal temperature. If it gets too warm during the test, take a layer off.

- **Get there on time** - The last thing you want to do is get to the test site late. Rather, you should be there 45 minutes prior to the start of the test. Upon your arrival, try not to hang out with anybody who is nervous. Any anxious energy they exhibit shouldn't influence you.

- **Leave the books at home** - No books should be brought to the test site. If you start developing anxiety before the test, books could encourage you to do some last-minute studying, which will only hinder you. Keep the books far away—better yet, leave them at home.

- **Make your voice heard** - If something is off, speak to a proctor. If medical attention is needed or if you'll require anything, consult the proctor prior to the start of the test. Any doubts you have should be clarified. You should be entering the test site with a state of mind that is completely clear.

- **Have faith in yourself** - When you feel confident, you will be able to perform at your best. When you are waiting for the test to begin, envision yourself receiving an outstanding result. Try to see yourself as someone who knows all the answers, no matter what the questions are. A lot of athletes tend to use this technique—particularly before a big competition. Your expectations will be reflected by your performance.

During your test

- **Be calm and breathe deeply** - You need to relax before the test, and some deep breathing will go a long way to help you do that. Be confident and calm. You got this. Everybody feels a little stressed out just before an evaluation of any kind is set to begin. Learn some effective breathing exercises. Spend a minute meditating before the test starts. Filter out any negative thoughts you have. Exhibit confidence when having such thoughts.

- **Concentrate on the test** - Refrain from comparing yourself to anyone else. You shouldn't be distracted by the people near you or random noise. Concentrate exclusively on the test. If you find yourself irritated by surrounding noises, earplugs can be used to block sounds off close to you. Don't forget—the test is going to last several hours if you're taking more than one subject of the test. Some of that time will be dedicated to brief sections. Concentrate on the specific section you are working on during a particular moment. Do not let your mind wander off to upcoming or previous sections.

- **Try to answer each question individually** - Focus only on the question you are working on. Use one of the test-taking strategies to solve the problem. If you aren't able to come up with an answer, don't get frustrated. Simply skip that question, then move onto the next one.

- **Don't forget to breathe!** Whenever you notice your mind wandering, your stress levels boosting, or frustration brewing, take a thirty-second break. Shut your eyes, drop your pencil, breathe deeply, and let your shoulders relax. You will end up being more productive when you allow yourself to relax for a moment.

- **Optimize your breaks** - When break time comes, use the restroom, have a snack, and reactivate your energy for the subsequent section. Doing some stretches can help stimulate your blood flow.

After your test

- **Take it easy** - You will need to set some time aside to relax and decompress once the test has concluded. There is no need to stress yourself out about what you could've said, or what you may have done wrong. At this point, there's nothing you can do about it. Your energy and time would be better spent on something that will bring you happiness for the remainder of your day.

- **Redoing the test** - Did you pass the test? Congratulations! Your hard work paid off!

  If you have failed your test, though, don't worry! The test can be retaken. In such cases, you will need to follow the retake policy. You also need to re-register to take the exam again.

Contents

Contents

Contents

Chapter 1: Fractions and Mixed Numbers

Math Topics that you'll learn in this Chapter:

- ✓ Simplifying Fractions
- ✓ Adding and Subtracting Fractions
- ✓ Multiplying and Dividing Fractions
- ✓ Adding Mixed Numbers
- ✓ Subtracting Mixed Numbers
- ✓ Multiplying Mixed Numbers
- ✓ Dividing Mixed Numbers

1

Simplifying Fractions

✏️ *Simplify each fraction.*

1) $\frac{8}{16} =$

2) $\frac{7}{21} =$

3) $\frac{11}{44} =$

4) $\frac{6}{24} =$

5) $\frac{6}{18} =$

6) $\frac{18}{27} =$

7) $\frac{15}{55} =$

8) $\frac{24}{54} =$

9) $\frac{63}{72} =$

10) $\frac{40}{64} =$

11) $\frac{23}{46} =$

12) $\frac{35}{63} =$

13) $\frac{32}{36} =$

14) $\frac{81}{99} =$

15) $\frac{16}{64} =$

16) $\frac{14}{35} =$

17) $\frac{19}{38} =$

18) $\frac{18}{54} =$

19) $\frac{56}{70} =$

20) $\frac{40}{45} =$

21) $\frac{9}{90} =$

22) $\frac{20}{25} =$

23) $\frac{36}{42} =$

24) $\frac{40}{48} =$

25) $\frac{18}{54} =$

26) $\frac{48}{144} =$

Adding and Subtracting Fractions

✎ *Calculate and write the answer in lowest term.*

1) $\frac{1}{3} + \frac{1}{5} =$

2) $\frac{2}{5} + \frac{3}{8} =$

3) $\frac{1}{3} - \frac{2}{9} =$

4) $\frac{4}{5} - \frac{2}{9} =$

5) $\frac{2}{9} + \frac{1}{3} =$

6) $\frac{3}{10} + \frac{2}{5} =$

7) $\frac{9}{10} - \frac{4}{5} =$

8) $\frac{7}{9} - \frac{3}{7} =$

9) $\frac{3}{4} + \frac{1}{3} =$

10) $\frac{3}{8} + \frac{2}{5} =$

11) $\frac{3}{4} - \frac{2}{5} =$

12) $\frac{7}{9} - \frac{2}{3} =$

13) $\frac{4}{9} + \frac{5}{6} =$

14) $\frac{2}{3} + \frac{1}{4} =$

15) $\frac{9}{10} - \frac{3}{5} =$

16) $\frac{7}{12} - \frac{1}{2} =$

17) $\frac{4}{5} + \frac{2}{3} =$

18) $\frac{5}{7} + \frac{1}{5} =$

19) $\frac{5}{9} - \frac{2}{5} =$

20) $\frac{3}{5} - \frac{2}{9} =$

21) $\frac{7}{9} + \frac{1}{7} =$

22) $\frac{5}{8} + \frac{2}{3} =$

23) $\frac{5}{7} - \frac{2}{5} =$

24) $\frac{7}{9} - \frac{3}{4} =$

25) $\frac{3}{5} - \frac{1}{6} =$

26) $\frac{3}{12} + \frac{2}{7} =$

Multiplying and Dividing Fractions

✍ *Solve and write the answer in lowest term.*

1) $\frac{1}{3} \times \frac{9}{5} =$

2) $\frac{1}{4} \times \frac{3}{7} =$

3) $\frac{1}{5} \div \frac{1}{4} =$

4) $\frac{1}{6} \div \frac{5}{12} =$

5) $\frac{2}{3} \times \frac{4}{7} =$

6) $\frac{5}{7} \times \frac{3}{4} =$

7) $\frac{2}{5} \div \frac{3}{7} =$

8) $\frac{3}{7} \div \frac{5}{8} =$

9) $\frac{3}{8} \times \frac{4}{7} =$

10) $\frac{2}{9} \times \frac{6}{11} =$

11) $\frac{1}{10} \div \frac{3}{8} =$

12) $\frac{3}{10} \div \frac{4}{5} =$

13) $\frac{6}{7} \times \frac{4}{9} =$

14) $\frac{3}{7} \times \frac{5}{6} =$

15) $\frac{7}{9} \div \frac{6}{11} =$

16) $\frac{1}{15} \div \frac{2}{3} =$

17) $\frac{1}{13} \times \frac{1}{2} =$

18) $\frac{1}{12} \times \frac{4}{7} =$

19) $\frac{1}{15} \div \frac{4}{9} =$

20) $\frac{1}{16} \div \frac{1}{2} =$

21) $\frac{4}{7} \times \frac{5}{8} =$

22) $\frac{1}{11} \times \frac{4}{5} =$

23) $\frac{1}{16} \div \frac{5}{8} =$

24) $\frac{1}{15} \div \frac{2}{3} =$

25) $\frac{1}{13} \times \frac{2}{5} =$

26) $\frac{1}{18} \times \frac{3}{7} =$

Chapter 1: Fractions and Mixed Numbers

Adding Mixed Numbers

✍ *Solve and write the answer in lowest terms.*

1) $1\frac{1}{5} + 2\frac{2}{5} =$

2) $1\frac{1}{2} + 4\frac{5}{6} =$

3) $2\frac{4}{5} + 2\frac{3}{10} =$

4) $3\frac{1}{6} + 2\frac{2}{5} =$

5) $1\frac{5}{6} + 1\frac{2}{5} =$

6) $3\frac{5}{7} + 1\frac{2}{9} =$

7) $3\frac{5}{8} + 2\frac{1}{3} =$

8) $1\frac{6}{7} + 3\frac{2}{9} =$

9) $2\frac{5}{9} + 1\frac{1}{4} =$

10) $3\frac{7}{9} + 2\frac{5}{6} =$

11) $2\frac{1}{10} + 2\frac{2}{5} =$

12) $1\frac{3}{10} + 3\frac{4}{5} =$

13) $3\frac{1}{12} + 2\frac{1}{3} =$

14) $5\frac{1}{11} + 1\frac{1}{2} =$

15) $3\frac{1}{21} + 2\frac{2}{3} =$

16) $4\frac{1}{24} + 1\frac{5}{8} =$

17) $2\frac{1}{25} + 3\frac{3}{5} =$

18) $3\frac{1}{15} + 2\frac{2}{10} =$

19) $5\frac{6}{7} + 2\frac{1}{3} =$

20) $2\frac{1}{8} + 3\frac{3}{4} =$

21) $2\frac{5}{7} + 2\frac{2}{21} =$

22) $4\frac{1}{6} + 1\frac{4}{5} =$

23) $2\frac{1}{7} + 2\frac{3}{8} =$

24) $3\frac{1}{4} + 2\frac{2}{3} =$

25) $1\frac{1}{13} + 2\frac{3}{4} =$

26) $3\frac{2}{35} + 2\frac{5}{7} =$

Subtracting Mixed Numbers

✎ *Solve and write the answer in lowest terms.*

1) $5\frac{2}{9} - 2\frac{1}{9} =$

2) $6\frac{2}{7} - 2\frac{1}{3} =$

3) $5\frac{3}{8} - 2\frac{3}{4} =$

4) $7\frac{2}{5} - 3\frac{1}{10} =$

5) $9\frac{5}{7} - 7\frac{4}{21} =$

6) $11\frac{7}{12} - 9\frac{5}{6} =$

7) $9\frac{5}{9} - 8\frac{1}{8} =$

8) $13\frac{7}{9} - 11\frac{3}{7} =$

9) $8\frac{7}{12} - 7\frac{3}{8} =$

10) $11\frac{5}{9} - 9\frac{1}{4} =$

11) $6\frac{5}{6} - 2\frac{2}{9} =$

12) $5\frac{7}{8} - 4\frac{1}{3} =$

13) $9\frac{5}{8} - 8\frac{1}{2} =$

14) $4\frac{9}{16} - 2\frac{1}{4} =$

15) $3\frac{2}{3} - 1\frac{2}{15} =$

16) $5\frac{1}{2} - 4\frac{2}{17} =$

17) $5\frac{6}{7} - 2\frac{1}{3} =$

18) $3\frac{3}{7} - 2\frac{2}{21} =$

19) $7\frac{3}{10} - 5\frac{2}{15} =$

20) $4\frac{5}{6} - 2\frac{2}{9} =$

21) $6\frac{3}{7} - 2\frac{2}{9} =$

22) $7\frac{4}{5} - 6\frac{3}{7} =$

23) $12\frac{3}{7} - 8\frac{1}{3} =$

24) $5\frac{4}{9} - 2\frac{5}{6} =$

25) $10\frac{1}{28} - 7\frac{3}{4} =$

26) $11\frac{5}{12} - 7\frac{5}{48} =$

Chapter 1: Fractions and Mixed Numbers

Multiplying Mixed Numbers

✏ *Solve and write the answer in lowest terms.*

1) $1\frac{1}{6} \times 1\frac{3}{7} =$

2) $5\frac{1}{6} \times 2\frac{1}{4} =$

3) $3\frac{3}{7} \times 1\frac{2}{9} =$

4) $3\frac{3}{8} \times 3\frac{1}{6} =$

5) $1\frac{1}{2} \times 5\frac{2}{3} =$

6) $3\frac{1}{2} \times 6\frac{2}{3} =$

7) $9\frac{1}{2} \times 2\frac{1}{6} =$

8) $2\frac{5}{8} \times 8\frac{3}{5} =$

9) $3\frac{4}{5} \times 4\frac{2}{3} =$

10) $5\frac{1}{3} \times 2\frac{2}{7} =$

11) $6\frac{1}{3} \times 3\frac{3}{4} =$

12) $7\frac{2}{3} \times 1\frac{8}{9} =$

13) $8\frac{1}{2} \times 2\frac{1}{6} =$

14) $4\frac{1}{5} \times 8\frac{2}{3} =$

15) $3\frac{1}{8} \times 5\frac{2}{3} =$

16) $2\frac{2}{7} \times 6\frac{2}{5} =$

17) $2\frac{3}{8} \times 7\frac{2}{3} =$

18) $1\frac{7}{8} \times 8\frac{2}{3} =$

19) $9\frac{1}{2} \times 3\frac{1}{5} =$

20) $2\frac{5}{8} \times 4\frac{1}{3} =$

21) $6\frac{1}{3} \times 3\frac{2}{5} =$

22) $5\frac{3}{4} \times 2\frac{2}{7} =$

23) $8\frac{1}{6} \times 2\frac{2}{7} =$

24) $4\frac{1}{6} \times 7\frac{1}{5} =$

25) $2\frac{1}{5} \times 2\frac{5}{8} =$

26) $6\frac{2}{3} \times 4\frac{3}{5} =$

Dividing Mixed Numbers

✍ *Solve and write the answer in lowest terms.*

1) $6\frac{1}{2} \div 4\frac{2}{5} =$

2) $1\frac{3}{8} \div 1\frac{1}{4} =$

3) $6\frac{2}{5} \div 2\frac{4}{5} =$

4) $7\frac{1}{3} \div 6\frac{3}{4} =$

5) $7\frac{2}{5} \div 3\frac{3}{4} =$

6) $2\frac{4}{5} \div 3\frac{2}{3} =$

7) $8\frac{3}{5} \div 4\frac{3}{4} =$

8) $6\frac{3}{4} \div 2\frac{2}{9} =$

9) $5\frac{2}{7} \div 2\frac{2}{9} =$

10) $2\frac{2}{5} \div 3\frac{3}{5} =$

11) $4\frac{3}{7} \div 1\frac{7}{8} =$

12) $2\frac{5}{7} \div 2\frac{4}{5} =$

13) $8\frac{3}{5} \div 6\frac{1}{5} =$

14) $2\frac{5}{8} \div 1\frac{8}{9} =$

15) $5\frac{6}{7} \div 2\frac{3}{4} =$

16) $1\frac{3}{5} \div 2\frac{3}{8} =$

17) $5\frac{3}{4} \div 3\frac{2}{5} =$

18) $2\frac{3}{4} \div 3\frac{1}{5} =$

19) $3\frac{2}{3} \div 1\frac{2}{5} =$

20) $4\frac{1}{4} \div 2\frac{2}{3} =$

21) $3\frac{5}{6} \div 2\frac{4}{5} =$

22) $2\frac{1}{8} \div 1\frac{3}{4} =$

23) $5\frac{1}{2} \div 4\frac{2}{5} =$

24) $6\frac{3}{7} \div 2\frac{1}{7} =$

25) $3\frac{3}{6} \div 1\frac{5}{7} =$

26) $4\frac{4}{9} \div 4\frac{2}{3} =$

Answers – Chapter 1

Simplifying Fractions

1) $\frac{1}{2}$

2) $\frac{1}{3}$

3) $\frac{1}{4}$

4) $\frac{1}{4}$

5) $\frac{1}{3}$

6) $\frac{2}{3}$

7) $\frac{3}{11}$

8) $\frac{4}{9}$

9) $\frac{7}{8}$

10) $\frac{5}{8}$

11) $\frac{1}{2}$

12) $\frac{5}{9}$

13) $\frac{8}{9}$

14) $\frac{9}{11}$

15) $\frac{1}{4}$

16) $\frac{2}{5}$

17) $\frac{1}{2}$

18) $\frac{1}{3}$

19) $\frac{4}{5}$

20) $\frac{8}{9}$

21) $\frac{1}{10}$

22) $\frac{4}{5}$

23) $\frac{6}{7}$

24) $\frac{5}{6}$

25) $\frac{1}{3}$

26) $\frac{1}{3}$

Adding and Subtracting Fractions

1) $\frac{8}{15}$

2) $\frac{31}{40}$

3) $\frac{1}{9}$

4) $\frac{26}{45}$

5) $\frac{5}{9}$

6) $\frac{7}{10}$

7) $\frac{1}{10}$

8) $\frac{22}{63}$

9) $\frac{13}{12}$

10) $\frac{31}{40}$

11) $\frac{7}{20}$

12) $\frac{1}{9}$

13) $\frac{23}{18}$

14) $\frac{11}{12}$

15) $\frac{3}{10}$

16) $\frac{1}{12}$

17) $\frac{22}{15}$

18) $\frac{32}{35}$

19) $\frac{7}{45}$

20) $\frac{17}{45}$

21) $\frac{58}{63}$

22) $\frac{31}{24}$

23) $\frac{11}{35}$

24) $\frac{1}{36}$

25) $\frac{13}{30}$

26) $\frac{15}{28}$

Multiplying and Dividing Fractions

1) $\frac{3}{5}$

2) $\frac{3}{28}$

3) $\frac{4}{5}$

4) $\frac{2}{5}$

5) $\frac{8}{21}$

6) $\frac{15}{28}$

7) $\frac{14}{15}$

8) $\frac{24}{35}$

9) $\frac{3}{14}$

10) $\frac{4}{33}$

11) $\frac{4}{15}$

12) $\frac{3}{8}$

13) $\frac{8}{21}$

14) $\frac{5}{14}$

15) $\frac{77}{54}$

16) $\frac{1}{10}$

17) $\frac{1}{26}$

18) $\frac{1}{21}$

19) $\frac{3}{20}$

20) $\frac{1}{8}$

21) $\frac{5}{14}$

22) $\frac{4}{55}$

23) $\frac{1}{10}$

24) $\frac{1}{10}$

25) $\frac{2}{65}$

26) $\frac{1}{42}$

Adding Mixed Numbers

1) $3\frac{3}{5}$

2) $6\frac{1}{3}$

3) $5\frac{1}{10}$

4) $5\frac{17}{30}$

5) $3\frac{7}{30}$

6) $4\frac{59}{63}$

7) $5\frac{23}{24}$

8) $5\frac{5}{63}$

9) $3\frac{29}{36}$

10) $6\frac{11}{18}$

11) $4\frac{1}{2}$

12) $5\frac{1}{10}$

13) $5\frac{5}{12}$

14) $6\frac{13}{22}$

15) $5\frac{5}{7}$

16) $5\frac{2}{3}$

17) $5\frac{16}{25}$

18) $5\frac{4}{15}$

19) $8\frac{4}{21}$

20) $5\frac{7}{8}$

21) $4\frac{17}{21}$

22) $5\frac{29}{30}$

23) $4\frac{29}{56}$

24) $5\frac{11}{12}$

25) $3\frac{43}{52}$

26) $5\frac{27}{35}$

Subtracting Mixed Numbers

1) $3\frac{1}{9}$

2) $3\frac{20}{21}$

3) $2\frac{5}{8}$

4) $4\frac{3}{10}$

5) $2\frac{11}{21}$

6) $1\frac{3}{4}$

7) $1\frac{31}{72}$

8) $2\frac{22}{63}$

9) $1\frac{5}{24}$

10) $2\frac{11}{36}$

11) $4\frac{11}{18}$

12) $1\frac{13}{24}$

13) $1\frac{1}{8}$

14) $2\frac{5}{16}$

15) $2\frac{8}{15}$

16) $1\frac{13}{34}$

17) $3\frac{11}{21}$

18) $1\frac{1}{3}$

19) $2\frac{1}{6}$

20) $2\frac{11}{18}$

21) $4\frac{13}{63}$

22) $1\frac{13}{35}$

23) $4\frac{2}{21}$

24) $2\frac{11}{18}$

25) $2\frac{2}{7}$

26) $4\frac{5}{16}$

Multiplying Mixed Numbers

1) $1\frac{2}{3}$

2) $11\frac{5}{8}$

3) $4\frac{4}{21}$

4) $10\frac{11}{16}$

5) $8\frac{1}{2}$

6) $23\frac{1}{3}$

7) $20\frac{7}{12}$

8) $22\frac{23}{40}$

9) $17\frac{11}{15}$

10) $12\frac{4}{21}$

11) $23\frac{3}{4}$

12) $14\frac{13}{27}$

13) $18\frac{5}{12}$

14) $36\frac{2}{5}$

15) $17\frac{17}{24}$

16) $14\frac{22}{35}$

17) $18\frac{5}{24}$

18) $16\frac{1}{4}$

19) $30\frac{2}{5}$

20) $11\frac{3}{8}$

21) $21\frac{8}{15}$

22) $13\frac{1}{7}$

23) $18\frac{2}{3}$

24) 30

25) $5\frac{31}{40}$

26) $30\frac{2}{3}$

Dividing Mixed Numbers

1) $1\frac{21}{44}$

2) $1\frac{1}{10}$

3) $2\frac{2}{7}$

4) $1\frac{7}{81}$

5) $1\frac{73}{75}$

6) $\frac{42}{55}$

7) $1\frac{77}{95}$

8) $3\frac{3}{80}$

9) $2\frac{53}{140}$

10) $\frac{2}{3}$

11) $2\frac{88}{105}$

12) $\frac{95}{98}$

13) $1\frac{12}{31}$

14) $1\frac{53}{136}$

15) $2\frac{10}{77}$

16) $\frac{64}{95}$

17) $1\frac{47}{68}$

18) $\frac{55}{64}$

19) $2\frac{13}{21}$

20) $1\frac{19}{32}$

21) $1\frac{31}{84}$

22) $1\frac{3}{14}$

23) $1\frac{1}{4}$

24) 3

25) $2\frac{1}{24}$

26) $\frac{20}{21}$

Chapter 2: Decimal

Math Topics that you'll learn in this Chapter:

- ✓ Comparing Decimals
- ✓ Rounding Decimals
- ✓ Adding and Subtracting Decimals
- ✓ Multiplying and Dividing Decimals

13

Comparing Decimals

✍ *Compare. Use >, =, and <*

1) 0.44 ☐ 0.044

2) 0.67 ☐ 0.68

3) 0.49 ☐ 0.79

4) 1.35 ☐ 1.45

5) 1.58 ☐ 1.75

6) 2.91 ☐ 2.85

7) 14.56 ☐ 1.456

8) 17.85 ☐ 17.89

9) 21.52 ☐ 21.052

10) 11.12 ☐ 11.03

11) 9.650 ☐ 9.65

12) 8.578 ☐ 8.568

13) 3.15 ☐ 0.315

14) 16.61 ☐ 16.16

15) 18.581 ☐ 8.991

16) 25.05 ☐ 2.505

17) 4.55 ☐ 4.65

18) 0.158 ☐ 1.58

19) 0.881 ☐ 0.871

20) 0.505 ☐ 0.510

21) 0.772 ☐ 0.777

22) 0.5 ☐ 0.500

23) 16.89 ☐ 15.89

24) 12.25 ☐ 12.35

25) 5.82 ☐ 5.69

26) 1.320 ☐ 1.032

27) 0.082 ☐ 0.088

28) 0.99 ☐ 0.099

29) 2.360 ☐ 2.840

30) 0.330 ☐ 0.303

31) 16.44 ☐ 1.664

32) 0.424 ☐ 0.442

Rounding Decimals

✍ *Round each number to the underlined place value.*

1) 3.960 =

2) 4.372 =

3) 11.136 =

4) 17.5 =

5) 1.981 =

6) 14.215 =

7) 17.548 =

8) 25.508 =

9) 31.089 =

10) 69.345 =

11) 9.457 =

12) 12.901 =

13) 2.658 =

14) 32.565 =

15) 6.058 =

16) 98.108 =

17) 27.705 =

18) 36.75 =

19) 9.08 =

20) 7.185 =

21) 22.547 =

22) 66.098 =

23) 87.75 =

24) 18.541 =

25) 10.258 =

26) 13.456 =

27) 71.084 =

28) 29.23 =

29) 43.45 =

30) 81.07 =

31) 92.366 =

32) 24.76 =

Adding and Subtracting Decimals

✎ *Solve.*

1) $11.62 + 18.23 =$

2) $13.78 + 16.58 =$

3) $56.30 - 45.68 =$

4) $59.36 - 30.88 =$

5) $24.32 + 26.45 =$

6) $36.25 + 18.37 =$

7) $47.85 - 35.12 =$

8) $85.65 - 67.48 =$

9) $25.49 + 34.18 =$

10) $19.99 + 48.66 =$

11) $46.32 - 27.77 =$

12) $54.62 - 48.12 =$

13) $24.42 + 16.54 =$

14) $52.13 + 12.32 =$

15) $82.36 - 78.65 =$

16) $64.12 - 49.15 =$

17) $36.41 + 24.52 =$

18) $85.96 - 74.63 =$

19) $52.62 - 42.54 =$

20) $21.20 + 24.58 =$

21) $32.15 + 17.17 =$

22) $96.32 - 85.54 =$

23) $89.78 - 69.85 =$

24) $29.28 + 39.79 =$

25) $11.11 + 19.99 =$

26) $28.82 + 20.88 =$

27) $63.14 - 28.91 =$

28) $56.61 - 49.72 =$

29) $66.14 + 32.12 =$

30) $30.19 + 25.83 =$

31) $68.21 - 25.10 =$

32) $76.57 - 45.13 =$

Multiplying and Dividing Decimals

✎ *Solve.*

1) $12.3 \times 0.2 =$

2) $12.6 \times 0.9 =$

3) $54.4 \div 2 =$

4) $64.8 \div 8 =$

5) $23.1 \times 0.3 =$

6) $1.2 \times 0.7 =$

7) $5.5 \div 0.5 =$

8) $64.8 \div 8 =$

9) $1.4 \times 0.5 =$

10) $4.5 \times 0.3 =$

11) $88.8 \div 4 =$

12) $10.5 \div 5 =$

13) $2.2 \times 0.3 =$

14) $0.2 \times 0.52 =$

15) $95.7 \div 100 =$

16) $36.6 \div 6 =$

17) $3.2 \times 2 =$

18) $4.1 \times 0.5 =$

19) $68.4 \div 2 =$

20) $27.9 \div 9 =$

21) $3.5 \times 4 =$

22) $4.8 \times 0.5 =$

23) $6.4 \div 4 =$

24) $72.8 \div 0.8 =$

25) $1.8 \times 3 =$

26) $6.5 \times 0.2 =$

27) $93.6 \div 3 =$

28) $45.15 \div 0.5 =$

29) $12.6 \times 0.5 =$

30) $13.2 \times 6 =$

31) $6.4 \div 0.8 =$

32) $98.6 \div 0.2 =$

Answers – Chapter 2

Comparing Decimals

1) $0.44 > 0.044$

2) $0.67 < 0.68$

3) $0.49 < 0.79$

4) $1.35 < 1.45$

5) $1.58 < 1.75$

6) $2.91 > 2.85$

7) $14.56 > 1.456$

8) $17.85 < 17.89$

9) $21.52 > 21.052$

10) $11.12 > 11.03$

11) $9.650 = 9.65$

12) $8.578 > 8.568$

13) $3.15 > 0.315$

14) $16.61 > 16.16$

15) $18.581 > 8.991$

16) $25.05 > 2.505$

17) $4.55 < 4.65$

18) $0.158 < 1.58$

19) $0.881 > 0.871$

20) $0.505 < 0.510$

21) $0.772 < 0.777$

22) $0.5 = 0.500$

23) $16.89 > 15.89$

24) $12.25 < 12.35$

25) $5.82 > 5.69$

26) $1.320 > 1.032$

27) $0.082 < 0.088$

28) $0.99 > 0.099$

29) $2.360 < 2.840$

30) $0.330 > 0.303$

31) $16.44 > 1.664$

32) $0.424 < 0.442$

Rounding Decimals

1) <u>3</u>.960 = 4

2) 4.3<u>7</u>2 = 4.37

3) 11.1<u>3</u>6 = 11.14

4) 1<u>7</u>.5 = 18

5) 1.9<u>8</u>1 = 1.98

6) 14.<u>2</u>15 = 14.2

7) 17.5<u>4</u>8 = 17.55

8) 25.5<u>0</u>8 = 25.51

9) 3<u>1</u>.089 = 31

10) 69.<u>3</u>45 = 69.3

11) 9.4<u>5</u>7 = 9.46

12) 1<u>2</u>.901 = 13

13) 2.6<u>5</u>8 = 2.66

14) 32.<u>5</u>65 = 32.6

15) 6.0<u>5</u>8 = 6.06

16) 98.1<u>0</u>8 = 98.11

17) 27.<u>7</u>05 = 27.7

18) 3<u>6</u>.75 = 37

19) 9.<u>0</u>8 = 9.1

20) 7.<u>1</u>85 = 7.2

21) 22.5<u>4</u>7 = 22.55

22) 66.<u>0</u>98 = 66.1

23) 8<u>7</u>.75 = 88

24) 18.<u>5</u>41 = 18.5

25) 10.2<u>5</u>8 = 10.26

26) 13.<u>4</u>56 = 13.5

27) 71.0<u>8</u>4 = 71.08

28) 2<u>9</u>.23 = 29

29) 43.<u>4</u>5 = 43.5

30) 8<u>1</u>.07 = 81

31) 9<u>2</u>.366 = 92

32) 24.<u>7</u>6 = 24.8

Adding and Subtracting Decimals

1) 29.85	9) 59.67	17) 60.93	25) 31.1
2) 30.36	10) 68.65	18) 11.33	26) 49.7
3) 10.62	11) 18.55	19) 10.08	27) 34.23
4) 28.48	12) 6.5	20) 45.78	28) 6.89
5) 50.77	13) 40.96	21) 49.32	29) 98.26
6) 54.62	14) 64.45	22) 10.78	30) 56.02
7) 12.73	15) 3.71	23) 19.93	31) 43.11
8) 18.17	16) 14.97	24) 69.07	32) 31.44

Multiplying and Dividing Decimals

1) 2.46	9) 0.7	17) 6.4	25) 5.4
2) 11.34	10) 1.35	18) 2.05	26) 1.3
3) 27.2	11) 22.2	19) 34.2	27) 31.2
4) 8.1	12) 2.1	20) 3.1	28) 90.3
5) 6.93	13) 0.66	21) 14	29) 6.3
6) 0.84	14) 0.104	22) 2.4	30) 79.2
7) 11	15) 0.957	23) 1.6	31) 8
8) 8.1	16) 6.1	24) 91	32) 493

Chapter 3: Integers and Order of Operations

Math Topics that you'll learn in this Chapter:

- ✓ Adding and Subtracting Integers
- ✓ Multiplying and Dividing Integers
- ✓ Order of Operations
- ✓ Integers and Absolute Value

21

Chapter 3: Integers and Order of Operations

Adding and Subtracting Integers

✎ *Solve.*

1) $-(9) + 15 =$

2) $15 - (-11 - 9) =$

3) $(-10) + (-6) =$

4) $(-10) + (-6) + 7 =$

5) $-(23) + 19 =$

6) $(-7 + 5) - 9 =$

7) $28 + (-32) =$

8) $(-11) + (-9) + 5 =$

9) $25 - (8 - 7) =$

10) $-(29) + 17 =$

11) $(-38) + (-3) + 29 =$

12) $15 - (-7 + 9) =$

13) $24 - (8 - 2) =$

14) $(-7 + 4) - 9 =$

15) $(-17) + (-3) + 9 =$

16) $(-26) + (-7) + 8 =$

17) $(-9) + (-11) =$

18) $8 - (-23 - 13) =$

19) $(-16) + (-2) =$

20) $25 - (7 - 4) =$

21) $23 + (-12) =$

22) $(-18) + (-6) =$

23) $17 - (-21 - 7) =$

24) $-(28) - (-16) + 5 =$

25) $(-9 + 4) - 8 =$

26) $(-28) + (-6) + 17 =$

27) $-(21) - (-15) + 9 =$

28) $(-31) + (-6) =$

29) $(-18) + (-10) + 13 =$

30) $(-30) + (-11) + 12 =$

31) $-(28) - (-10) + 6 =$

32) $6 - (-16 - 11) =$

Multiplying and Dividing Integers

✎ *Solve.*

1) $(-6) \times (-7) =$

2) $8 \times (-5) =$

3) $48 \div (-8) =$

4) $(-72) \div 9 =$

5) $(4) \times (-6) =$

6) $(-9) \times (-11) =$

7) $(10) \div (-5) =$

8) $144 \div (-12) =$

9) $(10) \times (-2) =$

10) $(-8) \times (-2) \times 5 =$

11) $(8) \div (-2) =$

12) $45 \div (-15) =$

13) $(5) \times (-7) =$

14) $(-6) \times (-5) \times 4 =$

15) $(12) \div (-6) =$

16) $(14) \div (-7) =$

17) $196 \div (-14) =$

18) $(27 - 13) \times (-2) =$

19) $125 \div (-5) =$

20) $66 \div (-6) =$

21) $(-6) \times (-5) \times 3 =$

22) $(15 - 6) \times (-3) =$

23) $(32 - 24) \div (-4) =$

24) $72 \div (-6) =$

25) $(-14 + 8) \times (-7) =$

26) $(-3) \times (-9) \times 3 =$

27) $84 \div (-12) =$

28) $(-12) \times (-10) =$

29) $22 \times (-3) =$

30) $(-2) \times (-6) \times 5 =$

31) $(24) \div (-3) =$

32) $(-15) \div (3) =$

Order of Operation

✎ *Calculate.*

1) $16 + (30 \div 5) =$

2) $(3 \times 9) \div (-3) =$

3) $57 - (3 \times 8) =$

4) $(-12) \times (7 - 3) =$

5) $(18 - 7) \times (6) =$

6) $(6 \times 10) \div (12 + 3) =$

7) $(13 \times 2) - (24 \div 6) =$

8) $(-5) + (4 \times 3) + 8 =$

9) $(4 \times 2^3) + (16 - 9) =$

10) $(3^2 \times 7) \div (-2 + 1) =$

11) $[-2(48 \div 2^3)] - 6 =$

12) $(-4) + (7 \times 8) + 18 =$

13) $(3 \times 7) + (16 - 7) =$

14) $[3^3 \times (48 \div 2^3)] \div (-2) =$

15) $(14 \times 3) - (3^4 \div 9) =$

16) $(96 \div 12) \times (-3) =$

17) $(48 \div 2^2) \times (-2) =$

18) $(56 \div 7) \times (-5) =$

19) $(-2^2) + (7 \times 9) - 21 =$

20) $(2^4 - 9) \times (-6) =$

21) $[4^3 \times (50 \div 5^2)] \div (-16) =$

22) $(3^2 \times 4^2) \div (-4 + 2) =$

23) $6^2 - (-6 \times 4) + 3 =$

24) $4^2 - (5^2 \times 3) =$

25) $(-4) + (12^2 \div 3^2) - 7^2 =$

26) $(3^2 \times 5) + (-5^2 - 9) =$

27) $2[(3^2 \times 5) \times (-6)] =$

28) $(11^2 - 2^2) - (-7^2) =$

29) $(2^2 \times 5) - (64 \div 8) =$

30) $2[(3^2 \times 4) + (35 \div 5)] =$

31) $(4^2 \times 3) \div (-6) =$

32) $3^2[(4^3 \div 16) - (3^3 \div 27)] =$

Integers and Absolute Value

✏️ *Calculate.*

1) $4 - |6 - 10| =$

2) $|14| - \frac{|-18|}{3} =$

3) $\frac{|8 \times -8|}{4} \times \frac{|-20|}{5} =$

4) $|12 \times 3| + \frac{|-81|}{9} =$

5) $4 - |11 - 18| - |3| =$

6) $|18| - \frac{|-12|}{4} =$

7) $\frac{|5 \times -8|}{10} \times \frac{|-22|}{11} =$

8) $|9 \times 3| + \frac{|-36|}{4} =$

9) $|-42 + 7| \times \frac{|-2 \times 5|}{10} =$

10) $6 - |17 - 11| - |5| =$

11) $|13| - \frac{|-54|}{6} =$

12) $\frac{|9 \times -4|}{12} \times \frac{|-45|}{9} =$

13) $|-75 + 50| \times \frac{|-4 \times 5|}{5} =$

14) $\frac{|-26|}{13} \times \frac{|-32|}{8} =$

15) $14 - |8 - 18| - |-12| =$

16) $|29| - \frac{|-20|}{5} =$

17) $\frac{|3 \times 8|}{2} \times \frac{|-33|}{3} =$

18) $|-45 + 15| \times \frac{|-12 \times 5|}{6} =$

19) $\frac{|-50|}{5} \times \frac{|-77|}{11} =$

20) $12 - |2 - 7| - |15| =$

21) $|18| - \frac{|-45|}{15} =$

22) $\frac{|7 \times 8|}{4} \times \frac{|-48|}{12} =$

23) $\frac{|30 \times 2|}{3} \times |-12| =$

24) $\frac{|-36|}{9} \times \frac{|-80|}{8} =$

25) $|-30 + 9| \times \frac{|-8 \times 5|}{8} =$

26) $|16| - \frac{|-18|}{3} =$

27) $12 - |10 - 24| + |5| =$

28) $|-38 + 8| \times \frac{|-5 \times 6|}{10} =$

Answers – Chapter 3

Adding and Subtracting Integers

1) 6
2) 35
3) −16
4) −9
5) −4
6) −11
7) −4
8) −15

9) 24
10) −12
11) −12
12) 13
13) 18
14) −12
15) −11
16) −25

17) −20
18) 44
19) −18
20) 22
21) 11
22) −24
23) 45
24) −7

25) −13
26) −17
27) 3
28) −37
29) −15
30) −29
31) −12
32) 33

Multiplying and Dividing Integers

1) 42
2) −40
3) −6
4) −8
5) −24
6) 99
7) −2
8) −12

9) −20
10) 80
11) −4
12) −3
13) −35
14) 120
15) −2
16) −2

17) −14
18) −28
19) −25
20) −11
21) 90
22) −27
23) −2
24) −12

25) 42
26) 81
27) −7
28) 120
29) −66
30) 60
31) −8
32) −5

Order of Operation

1) 22	9) 39	17) −24	25) −37
2) −9	10) −63	18) −40	26) 11
3) 33	11) −18	19) 38	27) −540
4) −48	12) 70	20) −42	28) 166
5) 66	13) 30	21) −8	29) 12
6) 4	14) −81	22) −72	30) 86
7) 22	15) 33	23) 63	31) −8
8) 15	16) −24	24) −59	32) 27

Integers and Absolute Value

1) 0	8) 36	15) −8	22) 56
2) 8	9) 35	16) 25	23) 240
3) 64	10) −5	17) 132	24) 40
4) 45	11) 4	18) 300	25) 105
5) −6	12) 15	19) 70	26) 10
6) 15	13) 100	20) −8	27) 3
7) 8	14) 8	21) 15	28) 90

Chapter 4: Ratios and Proportions

Math Topics that you'll learn in this Chapter:

- ✓ Simplifying Ratios
- ✓ Proportional Ratios
- ✓ Similarity and Ratios
- ✓ Simple Interest

29

Simplifying Ratios

✎ *Simplify each ratio.*

1) $3 : 21 = $ ___ : ___

2) $4 : 16 = $ ___ : ___

3) $\frac{2}{28} = -$

4) $\frac{18}{45} = -$

5) $10 : 30 = $ ___ : ___

6) $5 : 30 = $ ___ : ___

7) $\frac{34}{38} = -$

8) $\frac{45}{63} = -$

9) $10 : 45 = $ ___ : ___

10) $20 : 30 = $ ___ : ___

11) $\frac{40}{64} = -$

12) $\frac{10}{110} = -$

13) $8 : 12 = $ ___ : ___

14) $16 : 20 = $ ___ : ___

15) $\frac{24}{48} = -$

16) $\frac{21}{77} = -$

17) $8 : 24 = $ ___ : ___

18) $9 \text{ to } 36 = $ ___ : ___

19) $\frac{64}{72} = -$

20) $\frac{45}{60} = -$

21) $12 : 15 = $ ___ : ___

22) $18 : 54 = $ ___ : ___

23) $\frac{36}{54} = -$

24) $\frac{48}{104} = -$

25) $12 : 48 = $ ___ : ___

26) $18 : 72 = $ ___ : ___

27) $\frac{15}{75} = -$

28) $\frac{46}{52} = -$

Proportional Ratios

✍ *Solve each proportion for* x.

1) $\frac{4}{7} = \frac{8}{x}, x =$ ____

2) $\frac{9}{12} = \frac{x}{8}, x =$ ____

3) $\frac{3}{5} = \frac{12}{x}, x =$ ____

4) $\frac{3}{10} = \frac{x}{50}, x =$ ____

5) $\frac{3}{11} = \frac{15}{x}, x =$ ____

6) $\frac{6}{15} = \frac{x}{45}, x =$ ____

7) $\frac{6}{19} = \frac{12}{x}, x =$ ____

8) $\frac{7}{16} = \frac{x}{32}, x =$ ____

9) $\frac{18}{21} = \frac{54}{x}, x =$ ____

10) $\frac{13}{15} = \frac{39}{x}, x =$ ____

11) $\frac{9}{13} = \frac{72}{x}, x =$ ____

12) $\frac{8}{30} = \frac{x}{180}, x =$ ____

13) $\frac{3}{19} = \frac{9}{x}, x =$ ____

14) $\frac{1}{3} = \frac{x}{90}, x =$ ____

15) $\frac{25}{45} = \frac{x}{9}, x =$ ____

16) $\frac{1}{6} = \frac{9}{x}, x =$ ____

17) $\frac{7}{9} = \frac{63}{x}, x =$ ____

18) $\frac{54}{72} = \frac{x}{8}, x =$ ____

19) $\frac{32}{40} = \frac{4}{x}, x =$ ____

20) $\frac{21}{42} = \frac{x}{6}, x =$ ____

21) $\frac{56}{72} = \frac{7}{x}, x =$ ____

22) $\frac{1}{14} = \frac{x}{42}, x =$ ____

23) $\frac{5}{7} = \frac{75}{x}, x =$ ____

24) $\frac{30}{48} = \frac{x}{8}, x =$ ____

25) $\frac{36}{88} = \frac{9}{x}, x =$ ____

26) $\frac{62}{68} = \frac{x}{34}, x =$ ____

27) $\frac{42}{60} = \frac{x}{10}, x =$ ____

28) $\frac{8}{9} = \frac{x}{108}, x =$ ____

29) $\frac{40}{6} = \frac{x}{3}, x =$ ____

30) $\frac{88}{121} = \frac{x}{11}, x =$ ____

31) $\frac{10}{24} = \frac{x}{48}, x =$ ____

32) $\frac{32}{80} = \frac{x}{10}, x =$ ____

Create Proportion

✍ *State if each pair of ratios form a proportion.*

1) $\frac{3}{8}$ and $\frac{24}{50}$

2) $\frac{3}{11}$ and $\frac{6}{22}$

3) $\frac{4}{5}$ and $\frac{16}{20}$

4) $\frac{5}{11}$ and $\frac{12}{33}$

5) $\frac{5}{10}$ and $\frac{15}{30}$

6) $\frac{4}{13}$ and $\frac{8}{24}$

7) $\frac{6}{9}$ and $\frac{24}{36}$

8) $\frac{7}{12}$ and $\frac{14}{20}$

9) $\frac{3}{8}$ and $\frac{27}{72}$

10) $\frac{12}{20}$ and $\frac{36}{60}$

11) $\frac{11}{12}$ and $\frac{55}{60}$

12) $\frac{12}{15}$ and $\frac{24}{25}$

13) $\frac{15}{19}$ and $\frac{20}{38}$

14) $\frac{10}{14}$ and $\frac{40}{56}$

15) $\frac{11}{13}$ and $\frac{44}{39}$

16) $\frac{15}{16}$ and $\frac{30}{32}$

17) $\frac{17}{19}$ and $\frac{34}{48}$

18) $\frac{5}{18}$ and $\frac{15}{54}$

19) $\frac{3}{14}$ and $\frac{18}{42}$

20) $\frac{7}{11}$ and $\frac{14}{32}$

21) $\frac{8}{11}$ and $\frac{32}{44}$

22) $\frac{8}{14}$ and $\frac{24}{54}$

✍ *Solve.*

23) The ratio of boys to girls in a class is 3: 4. If there are 27 boys in the class, how many girls are in that class? _____

24) The ratio of red marbles to blue marbles in a bag is 5: 6. If there are 66 marbles in the bag, how many of the marbles are red? _____

25) You can buy 6 cans of green beans at a supermarket for $3.60. How much does it cost to buy 48 cans of green beans? _____

Similarity and Ratios

✎ *Each pair of figures is similar. Find the missing side.*

Chapter 4: Ratios and Proportions

Simple Interest

✍ *Determine the simple interest for these loans.*

1) $400 at 6% for 4 years. $___

2) $580 at 3.5% for 5 years. $_

3) $320 at 4% for 6 years. $___

4) $510 at 8% for 3 years. $___

5) $690 at 5% for 6 months. $___

6) $620 at 7% for 3 years. $___

7) $650 at 4.5% for 10 years. $___

8) $850 at 4% for 2 years. $___

9) $640 at 7% for 3 years. $___

10) $300 at 9% for 9 months. $___

11) $760 at 8% for 2 years. $_

12) $910 at 5% for 5 years. $___

13) $540 at 3% for 6 years. $___

14) $780 at 2.5% for 4 years. $___

15) $1,600 at 7% for 3 months. $___

16) $310 at 4% for 4 years. $___

17) $950 at 6% for 5 years. $___

18) $280 at 8% for 7 years. $___

19) $310 at 6% for 3 years. $___

20) $990 at 5% for 4 months. $___

21) $380 at 6% for 5 years. $___

22) $580 at 6% for 4 years. $___

23) $1,200 at 4% for 5 years. $___

24) $3,100 at 5% for 6 years. $___

25) $5,200 at 8% for 2 years. $___

26) $1,400 at 4% for 3 years. $___

27) $300 at 3% for 8 months. $___

28) $150 at 3.5% for 4 years. $___

29) $170 at 6% for 2 years. $___

30) $940 at 8% for 5 years. $___

31) $960 at 1.5% for 8 years. $_

32) $240 at 5% for 4 months. $___

33) $280 at 2% for 5 years. $___

34) $880 at 3% for 2 years. $___

35) $2,200 at 4.5% for 2 years. $___

36) $2,400 at 7% for 3 years. $___

37) $1,800 at 5% for 6 months. $___

38) $190 at 4% for 2 years. $___

39) $480 at 6% for 5 years. $___

40) $700 at 5% for 6 years. $_

Answers – Chapter 4

Simplifying Ratios

1) $1:7$

2) $1:4$

3) $\dfrac{1}{14}$

4) $\dfrac{2}{5}$

5) $1:3$

6) $1:6$

7) $\dfrac{17}{19}$

8) $\dfrac{5}{7}$

9) $2:9$

10) $2:3$

11) $\dfrac{5}{8}$

12) $\dfrac{1}{11}$

13) $2:3$

14) $4:5$

15) $\dfrac{1}{2}$

16) $\dfrac{3}{11}$

17) $1:3$

18) 1 to 4

19) $\dfrac{8}{9}$

20) $\dfrac{3}{4}$

21) $4:5$

22) $1:3$

23) $\dfrac{2}{3}$

24) $\dfrac{6}{13}$

25) $1:4$

26) $1:4$

27) $\dfrac{1}{5}$

28) $\dfrac{23}{26}$

Proportional Ratios

1) $x = 14$

2) $x = 6$

3) $x = 20$

4) $x = 15$

5) $x = 55$

6) $x = 18$

7) $x = 38$

8) $x = 14$

9) $x = 63$

10) $x = 45$

11) $x = 104$

12) $x = 48$

13) $x = 57$

14) $x = 30$

15) $x = 5$

16) $x = 54$

17) $x = 81$

18) $x = 6$

19) $x = 5$

20) $x = 3$

21) $x = 9$

22) $x = 3$

23) $x = 105$

24) $x = 5$

25) $x = 22$

26) $x = 31$

27) $x = 7$

28) $x = 96$

29) $x = 20$

30) $x = 8$

31) $x = 20$

32) $x = 4$

Create Proportion

1) *No*

2) *Yes*

3) *Yes*

4) *No*

5) *Yes*

6) *No*

7) *Yes*

8) *No*

9) *Yes*

10) *Yes*

11) *Yes*

12) *No*

13) *No*

14) *Yes*

15) *No*

16) *Yes*

17) *No*

18) *Yes*

19) *No*

20) *No*

21) *Yes*

22) *No*

23) 36 *girls*

24) 30 *red marbles*

25) $28.80

Similarity and Ratios

1) 5

2) 18

3) 3

4) 32

5) 9

6) 8

7) 12

8) 16

Simple Interest

1) $96	15) $28	29) $20.40
2) $101.50	16) $49.60	30) $376
3) $76.80	17) $285	31) $115.20
4) $122.40	18) $156.80	32) $4
5) $17.25	19) $55.80	33) $28
6) $130.20	20) $16.5	34) $52.80
7) $292.50	21) $114	35) $198
8) $68	22) $139.20	36) $504
9) $134.40	23) $240	37) $45
10) $20.25	24) $930	38) $15.20
11) $121.60	25) $832	39) $144
12) $227.50	26) $168	40) $210
13) $97.20	27) $6	
14) $78	28) $21	

Chapter 5:
Percentage

Math Topics that you'll learn in this Chapter:

- ✓ Percent Problems
- ✓ Percent of Increase and Decrease
- ✓ Discount, Tax and Tip

39

Percent Problems

Solve each problem.

1) What is 4 percent of 280? ____

2) What is 25 percent of 500? ____

3) What is 10 percent of 460? ____

4) What is 34 percent of 260? ____

5) What is 60 percent of 850? ____

6) 63 is what percent of 300? ____%

7) 80 is what percent of 400? ____%

8) 70 is what percent of 700? ____%

9) 84 is what percent of 600? ___%

10) 90 is what percent of 300? ___%

11) 24 is what percent of 150? ___%

12) 12 is what percent of 80? ____%

13) 4 is what percent of 50? ____%

14) 110 is what percent of 500? _%

15) 16 is what percent of 400? __%

16) 39 is what percent of 300? ___%

17) 56 is what percent of 200? ___%

18) 30 is what percent of 500? ___%

19) 84 is what percent of 700? ___%

20) 40 is what percent of 500? __%

21) 26 is what percent of 100? __ %

22) 45 is what percent of 900? __%

23) 60 is what percent of 400? ___%

24) 18 is what percent of 900? ___%

25) 75 is what percent of 250? ___%

26) 27 is what percent of 900? ___%

27) 49 is what percent of 700? ___%

28) 81 is what percent of 900? ___%

29) 90 is what percent of 500? ___%

30) 82 is what percent of 410? ___%

31) 14 is 35 percent of what number? ____

32) 90 is 6 percent of what number? ____

33) 80 is 40 percent of what number? ____

34) 80 is 20 percent of what number? ____

35) 30 is 6 percent of what number? ____

36) 64 is 8 percent of what number? ____

Chapter 5: Percentage

Percent of Increase and Decrease

✎ *Solve each percent of change word problem.*

1) Bob got a raise, and his hourly wage increased from $30 to $42. What is the percent increase? _____ %

2) The price of gasoline rose from $4.40 to $4.62 in one month. By what percent did the gas price rise? _____ %

3) In a class, the number of students has been increased from 25 to 32. What is the percent increase? _____ %

4) The price of a pair of shoes increases from $24 to $30. What is the percent increase? ____ %

5) In a class, the number of students has been decreased from 24 to 18. What is the percentage decrease? _____ %

6) Nick got a raise, and his hourly wage increased from $50 to $55. What is the percent increase? _____ %

7) A coat was originally priced at $60. It went on sale for $54. What was the percent that the coat was discounted? _____ %

8) The price of a pair of shoes increases from $12 to $18. What is the percent increase? ____ %

9) A house was purchased in 2002 for $150,000. It is now valued at $132,000. What is the rate (percent) of depreciation for the house?_____ %

10) The price of gasoline rose from $4.00 to $4.20 in one month. By what percent did the gas price rise? _____ %

Discount, Tax and Tip

✎ *Find the missing values.*

1) Original price of a computer: $540, Tax: 6%, Selling price: $_____

2) Original price of a sofa: $400, Tax: 14%, Selling price: $_____

3) Original price of a table: $560, Tax: 15%, Selling price: $_____

4) Original price of a cell phone: $740, Tax: 24%, Selling price: $_____

5) Original price of a printer: $400, Tax: 22%, Selling price: $_____

6) Original price of a computer: $600, Tax: 15%, Selling price: $_____

7) Restaurant bill: $24.00, Tip: 25%, Final amount: $_____

8) Original price of a cell phone: $300 Tax: 8%, Selling price: $_____

9) Original price of a carpet: $800, Tax: 25%, Selling price: $_____

10) Original price of a camera: $200 Discount: 35%, Selling price: $_____

11) Original price of a dress: $560 Discount: 10%, Selling price: $___

12) Original price of a monitor: $420 Discount: 6%, Selling price: $____

13) Original price of a laptop: $880 Discount: 16%, Selling price: $____

14) Restaurant bill: $64.00, Tip: 20%, Final amount: $____

Answers – Chapter 5

Percent Problems

1) 11.2

2) 125

3) 46

4) 88.4

5) 510

6) 21%

7) 20%

8) 10%

9) 14%

10) 30%

11) 16%

12) 15%

13) 8%

14) 22%

15) 4%

16) 13%

17) 28%

18) 6%

19) 12%

20) 8%

21) 26%

22) 5%

23) 15%

24) 2%

25) 30%

26) 3%

27) 7%

28) 9%

29) 18%

30) 20%

31) 40

32) 1,500

33) 200

34) 400

35) 500

36) 800

Percent of Increase and Decrease

1) 40%

2) 5%

3) 28%

4) 25%

5) 25%

6) 10%

7) 10%

8) 50%

9) 12%

10) 5%

Discount, Tax and Tip

1) $572.40	6) $690	11) $504
2) $456	7) $30.00	12) $394.8
3) $644	8) $324	13) $739.2
4) $917.60	9) $1,000	14) $76.80
5) $488	10) $130	

Chapter 6:
Expressions and Variables

Math Topics that you'll learn in this Chapter:

✓ Simplifying Variable Expressions

✓ Simplifying Polynomial Expressions

✓ Evaluating One Variable

✓ Evaluating Two Variables

✓ The Distributive Property

45

Simplifying Variable Expressions

✎ *Simplify and write the answer.*

1) $6x + 2 + 3x =$

2) $7x + 4 - 6x =$

3) $-1 - x^2 - 9x^2 =$

4) $(-5)(6x - 2) =$

5) $3 + 10x^2 + 2x =$

6) $8x^2 + 6x + 7x^2 =$

7) $2x^2 - 5x - 7x =$

8) $x - 3 + 5 - 3x =$

9) $2 - 3x + 12 - 2x =$

10) $5x^2 - 12x^2 + 8x =$

11) $2x^2 + 6x + 3x^2 =$

12) $2x^2 - 2x - x =$

13) $2x^2 - (-8x + 6) =$

14) $4x + 6(2 - 5x) =$

15) $10x + 8(10x - 6) =$

16) $9(-2x - 6) - 5 =$

17) $32x - 4 + 23 + 2x =$

18) $8x - 12x - x^2 + 13 =$

19) $(-6)(8x - 4) + 10x =$

20) $14x - 5(5 - 8x) =$

21) $23x + 4(9x + 3) + 12 =$

22) $3(-7x + 5) + 20x =$

23) $12x - 3x(x + 9) =$

24) $7x + 5x(3 - 3x) =$

25) $5x(-8x + 12) + 14x =$

26) $40x + 12 + 2x^2 =$

27) $5x(x - 3) - 10 =$

28) $8x - 7 + 8x + 2x^2 =$

29) $6x - 2x^2 - 6x^2 - 5 =$

30) $3 + x^2 - 4x^2 - 10x =$

31) $10x + 6x^2 + 5x + 18 =$

32) $20 + 12x^2 + 7x - 6x^2 =$

Simplifying Polynomial Expressions

✎ *Simplify and write the answer.*

1) $(3x^3 + 4x^2) - (10x + 3x^2) = $ _____

2) $(-4x^5 + 4x^3) - (6x^3 + 5x^2) = $ _____

3) $(10x^4 + 6x^2) - (x^2 - 8x^4) = $ _____

4) $6x - 2x^2 - 3(2x^2 + 5x^3) = $ _____

5) $(2x^3 - 3) + 3(2x^2 - 3x^3) = $ _____

6) $4(4x^3 - 2x) - (3x^3 - 2x^4) = $ _____

7) $2(4x - 3x^3) - 3(3x^3 + 4x^2) = $ _____

8) $(2x^2 - 2x) - (2x^3 + 5x^2) = $ _____

9) $2x^3 - (4x^4 + 2x) + x^2 = $ _____

10) $x^4 - 9(x^2 + x) - 5x = $ _____

11) $(-2x^2 - x^4) + (4x^4 - x^2) = $ _____

12) $4x^2 - 5x^3 + 15x^4 - 12x^3 = $ _____

13) $3x^2 - 2x^4 + 12x^4 - 10x^3 = $ _____

14) $4x^2 + 6x^3 - 8x^2 + 14x = $ _____

15) $3x^4 - 6x^5 + 7x^4 - 9x^2 = $ _____

16) $5x^3 + 15x - 4x^2 - 3x^3 = $ _____

Evaluating One Variable

✎ *Evaluate each expression using the value given.*

1) $x = 2 \Rightarrow 5x - 10 =$

2) $x = 3 \Rightarrow 6x - 12 =$

3) $x = 4 \Rightarrow 6x + 8 =$

4) $x = 6 \Rightarrow 2x + 4 =$

5) $x = 4 \Rightarrow 4x - 8 =$

6) $x = 2 \Rightarrow 5x - 2x + 10 =$

7) $x = 3 \Rightarrow 2x - x - 6 =$

8) $x = 4 \Rightarrow 6x - 3x + 4 =$

9) $x = -2 \Rightarrow 4x - 6x - 5 =$

10) $x = -1 \Rightarrow 3x - 5x + 11 =$

11) $x = 1 \Rightarrow x - 7x + 12 =$

12) $x = 2 \Rightarrow 2(-3x + 4) =$

13) $x = 3 \Rightarrow 4(-5x - 2) =$

14) $x = 2 \Rightarrow 5(-2x - 4) =$

15) $x = -2 \Rightarrow 3(-4x - 5) =$

16) $x = 3 \Rightarrow 8x + 5 =$

17) $x = -3 \Rightarrow 12x + 9 =$

18) $x = -1 \Rightarrow 9x - 8 =$

19) $x = 2 \Rightarrow 16x - 10 =$

20) $x = 1 \Rightarrow 4x + 3 =$

21) $x = 5 \Rightarrow 7x - 2 =$

22) $x = 7 \Rightarrow 28 - x =$

23) $x = 8 \Rightarrow 4x - 12 =$

24) $x = 10 \Rightarrow 44 - 3x =$

25) $x = 4 \Rightarrow 10x - 6 =$

26) $x = 7 \Rightarrow 6x - x + 9 =$

Evaluating Two Variables

✍ *Evaluate each expression using the values given.*

1) $x + 4y, x = 3, y = 2$ _____

2) $6x + 3y, x = -2, y = -3$ _____

3) $x + 5y, x = 2, y = -1$ _____

4) $3a - (10 - b), a = 3, b = 4$ _____

5) $4a - (6 - 3b), a = 1, b = 4$ _____

6) $a - (8 - 2b), a = 2, b = 5$ _____

7) $3z + 21 + 5k, z = 4, k = 1$ _____

8) $-7a + 4b, a = 6, b = 3$ _____

9) $-4a + 3b, a = 2, b = 4$ _____

10) $-6a + 6b, a = 4, b = 3$ _____

11) $-8a + 2b, a = 4, b = 6$ _____

12) $4x + 6y, x = 6, y = 3$ _____

13) $2x + 9y, x = 8, y = 1$ _____

14) $x - 7y, x = 9, y = 4$ _____

15) $5x - 4y, x = 6, y = 3$ _____

16) $2z + 14 + 8k, z = 4, k = 1$ _____

17) $6x + 3y, x = 3, y = 8$ _____

18) $5a - 6b, a = -3, b = -1$ _____

19) $6a + 2b, a = -6, b = 4$ _____

20) $-3a - b, a = 5, b = -6$ _____

21) $-6a + 2b, a = 6, b = -3$ _____

22) $-6a + 8b, a = 6, b = -1$ _____

The Distributive Property

✎ *Use the distributive property to simply each expression.*

1) $(-2)(10x + 3) =$

2) $(-3x + 5)(-5) =$

3) $11(-3x + 3) =$

4) $6(5 - 4x) =$

5) $(6 - 5x)(-4) =$

6) $9(8 - 2x) =$

7) $(-4x + 6)5 =$

8) $(-2x + 7)(-8) =$

9) $8(-4x + 7) =$

10) $(-9x + 5)(-3) =$

11) $8(-x + 9) =$

12) $7(2 - 6x) =$

13) $(-12x + 4)(-3) =$

14) $(-6)(-10x + 6) =$

15) $(-5)(5 - 11x) =$

16) $9(4 - 8x) =$

17) $(-6x + 2)7 =$

18) $(-9)(1 - 12x) =$

19) $(-3)(4 - 6x) =$

20) $(2 - 8x)(-2) =$

21) $20(2 - x) =$

22) $12(-4x + 3) =$

23) $12(3 - 4x) =$

24) $(-6x + 6)3 =$

25) $(-10x + 6)(-3) =$

26) $13(4 - 7x) =$

Answers – Chapter 6

Simplifying Variable Expressions

1) $9x + 2$

2) $x + 4$

3) $-10x^2 - 1$

4) $-30x + 10$

5) $10x^2 + 2x + 3$

6) $15x^2 + 6x$

7) $2x^2 - 12x$

8) $-2x + 2$

9) $-5x + 14$

10) $-7x^2 + 8x$

11) $5x^2 + 6x$

12) $2x^2 - 3x$

13) $2x^2 + 8x - 6$

14) $-26x + 12$

15) $90x - 48$

16) $-18x - 59$

17) $34x + 19$

18) $-x^2 - 4x + 13$

19) $-38x + 24$

20) $54x - 25$

21) $59x + 24$

22) $-x + 15$

23) $-3x^2 - 15x$

24) $-15x^2 + 22x$

25) $-40x^2 + 74x$

26) $2x^2 + 40x + 12$

27) $5x^2 - 15x - 10$

28) $2x^2 + 16x - 7$

29) $-8x^2 + 6x - 5$

30) $-3x^2 - 10x + 3$

31) $6x^2 + 15x + 18$

32) $6x^2 + 7x + 20$

Simplifying Polynomial Expressions

1) $3x^3 + x^2 - 10x$

2) $-4x^5 - 2x^3 - 5x^2$

3) $18x^4 + 5x^2$

4) $-15x^3 - 8x^2 + 6x$

5) $-7x^3 + 6x^2 - 3$

6) $2x^4 + 13x^3 - 8x$

7) $-15x^3 - 12x^2 + 8x$

8) $-2x^3 - 3x^2 - 2x$

9) $-4x^4 + 2x^3 + x^2 - 2x$

10) $x^4 - 9x^2 - 14x$

11) $3x^4 - 3x^2$

12) $15x^4 - 17x^3 + 4x^2$

13) $10x^4 - 10x^3 + 3x^2$

14) $6x^3 - 4x^2 + 14x$

15) $-6x^5 + 10x^4 - 9x^2$

16) $2x^3 - 4x^2 + 15x$

Evaluating One Variable

1) 0

2) 6

3) 32

4) 16

5) 8

6) 16

7) −3

8) 16

9) −1

10) 13

11) 6

12) −4

13) −68

14) −40

15) 9

16) 29

17) −27

18) −17

19) 22

20) 7

21) 33

22) 21

23) 20

24) 14

25) 34

26) 44

Evaluating Two Variables

1) 11

2) −21

3) −3

4) 3

5) 10

6) 4

7) 38

8) −30

9) 4

10) −6

11) −20

12) 42

13) 25

14) −19

15) 18

16) 30

17) 42

18) −9

19) −28

20) −9

21) −42

22) −44

The Distributive Property

1) $-20x - 6$

2) $15x - 25$

3) $-33x + 33$

4) $-24x + 30$

5) $20x - 24$

6) $-18x + 72$

7) $-20x + 30$

8) $16x - 56$

9) $-32x + 56$

10) $27x - 15$

11) $-8x + 72$

12) $-42x + 14$

13) $36x - 12$

14) $60x - 36$

15) $55x - 25$

16) $-72x + 36$

17) $-42x + 14$

18) $108x - 9$

19) $18x - 12$

20) $16x - 4$

21) $-20x + 40$

22) $-48x + 36$

23) $-48x + 36$

24) $-18x + 18$

25) $30x - 18$

26) $-91x + 52$

Chapter 7: Equations and Inequalities

Math Topics that you'll learn in this Chapter:

- ✓ One–Step Equations
- ✓ Multi–Step Equations
- ✓ System of Equations
- ✓ Graphing Single–Variable Inequalities
- ✓ One–Step Inequalities
- ✓ Multi–Step Inequalities

55

One–Step Equations

✎ *Solve each equation for x.*

1) $x - 18 = 28 \Rightarrow x = $ _____

2) $19 = -5 + x \Rightarrow x = $ _____

3) $15 - x = 6 \Rightarrow x = $ _____

4) $x - 24 = 29 \Rightarrow x = $ _____

5) $24 - x = 17 \Rightarrow x = $ _____

6) $16 - x = 3 \Rightarrow x = $ _____

7) $x + 14 = 12 \Rightarrow x = $ _____

8) $26 + x = 8 \Rightarrow x = $ _____

9) $x + 9 = -18 \Rightarrow x = $ _____

10) $x + 21 = 11 \Rightarrow x = $ _____

11) $17 = -5 + x \Rightarrow x = $ _____

12) $x + 20 = 29 \Rightarrow x = $ _____

13) $x - 13 = 19 \Rightarrow x = $ _____

14) $x + 9 = -17 \Rightarrow x = $ _____

15) $x + 4 = -23 \Rightarrow x = $ _____

16) $16 = -9 + x \Rightarrow x = $ _____

17) $4x = 28 \Rightarrow x = $ _____

18) $21 = -7x \Rightarrow x = $ _____

19) $12x = -12 \Rightarrow x = $ _____

20) $13x = 39 \Rightarrow x = $ _____

21) $8x = -16 \Rightarrow x = $ _____

22) $\frac{x}{2} = -5 \Rightarrow x = $ _____

23) $\frac{x}{9} = 6 \Rightarrow x = $ _____

24) $27 = \frac{x}{5} \Rightarrow x = $ _____

25) $\frac{x}{4} = -3 \Rightarrow x = $ _____

26) $x \div 8 = 7 \Rightarrow x = $ _____

27) $x \div 2 = -3 \Rightarrow x = $ _____

28) $8x = 56 \Rightarrow x = $ _____

29) $9x = 54 \Rightarrow x = $ _____

30) $7x = -35 \Rightarrow x = $ _____

31) $60 = -10x \Rightarrow x = $ _____

Multi –Step Equations

✎ *Solve each equation.*

1) $4x - 7 = 13 \Rightarrow x =$ _____

2) $26 = -(x - 4) \Rightarrow x =$ _____

3) $-(5 - x) = 19 \Rightarrow x =$ _____

4) $35 = -x + 14 \Rightarrow x =$ _____

5) $2(3 - 2x) = 10 \Rightarrow x =$ _____

6) $3x - 3 = 15 \Rightarrow x =$ _____

7) $32 = -x + 15 \Rightarrow x =$ _____

8) $-(10 - x) = -13 \Rightarrow x =$ _____

9) $-4(7 + x) = 4 \Rightarrow x =$ _____

10) $22 = 2x - 8 \Rightarrow x =$ _____

11) $-6(3 + x) = 6 \Rightarrow x =$ _____

12) $-3 = 3x - 15 \Rightarrow x =$ _____

13) $-7(12 + x) = 7 \Rightarrow x =$ _____

14) $8(6 - 4x) = 16 \Rightarrow x =$ _____

15) $18 - 4x = -9 - x \Rightarrow x =$ _____

16) $6(4 - x) = 30 \Rightarrow x =$ _____

17) $15 - 3x = -5 - x \Rightarrow x =$ _____

18) $9(-7 - 3x) = 18 \Rightarrow x =$ _____

19) $16 - 2x = -4 - 7x \Rightarrow x =$ _____

20) $14 - 2x = 14 + x \Rightarrow x =$ _____

21) $21 - 3x = -7 - 10x \Rightarrow x =$ __

22) $8 - 2x = 11 + x \Rightarrow x =$ _____

23) $10 + 12x = -8 + 6x =$ _____

24) $25 + 20x = -5 + 5x =$ _____

25) $16 - x = -8 - 7x \Rightarrow x =$ _____

26) $17 - 3x = 13 + x \Rightarrow x =$ _____

27) $22 + 5x = -8 - x \Rightarrow x =$ _____

28) $-9(7 + x) = 9 \Rightarrow x =$ _____

29) $12 + 2x = -4 - 2x \Rightarrow x =$ _____

30) $12 - x = 2 - 3x \Rightarrow x =$ _____

31) $19 - x = -1 - 11x \Rightarrow x =$ _____

32) $14 - 3x = -5 - 4x \Rightarrow x =$ _____

System of Equations

✏️ *Solve each system of equations.*

1) $2x + 3y = 15$ $x =$

    $x - 3y = 3$ $y =$

2) $y = x + 3$ $x =$

    $x + y = -5$ $y =$

3) $x + 3y = 6$ $x =$

    $2x + 8y = -12$ $y =$

4) $2x + y = 5$ $x =$

    $-3x + 6y = 0$ $y =$

5) $10x - 8y = -15$ $x =$

    $-6x + 4y = 13$ $y =$

6) $-3x - 4y = 5$ $x =$

    $x - 2y = 5$ $y =$

7) $5x - 12y = -19$ $x =$

    $-6x + 7y = 8$ $y =$

8) $5x - 7y = -2$ $x =$

    $-x - 2y = -3$ $y =$

9) $-x + 3y = 3$ $x =$

    $-7x + 8y = -5$ $y =$

10) $-4x + 3y = -18$ $x =$

    $4x - y = 14$ $y =$

11) $6x - 7y = -8$ $x =$

    $-x - 4y = -9$ $y =$

12) $-3x + 2y = -16$ $x =$

    $4x - y = 13$ $y =$

13) $2x + 3y = 8$ $x =$

    $-3x + 2y = 1$ $y =$

14) $y = -x + 3$ $x =$

    $3y + 5x = -1$ $y =$

15) $2x + 3y = 12$ $x =$

    $x + y = 5$ $y =$

16) $y = x - 1$ $x =$

    $y = 2x + 2$ $y =$

Graphing Single–Variable Inequalities

✍ *Graph each inequality.*

1) $x < 5$

2) $x \geq 2$

3) $x \geq -4$

4) $x \leq -1$

5) $x > -1$

6) $3 > x$

7) $2 \leq x$

8) $x > 0$

9) $-3 \leq x$

10) $-4 \leq x$

11) $x \leq 6$

12) $1 \leq x$

13) $-4 < x$

14) $x > -5$

One–Step Inequalities

✎ *Solve each inequality for* x.

1) $x - 9 < 20 \Rightarrow$ _____

2) $14 \leq -6 + x \Rightarrow$ _____

3) $x - 31 > 9 \Rightarrow$ _____

4) $x + 28 \geq 36 \Rightarrow$ _____

5) $x - 24 > 17 \Rightarrow$ _____

6) $x + 5 \geq 3 \Rightarrow x$_____

7) $x + 14 < 12 \Rightarrow$ _____

8) $26 + x \leq 8 \Rightarrow$ _____

9) $x + 9 \geq -18 \Rightarrow$ _____

10) $x + 24 < 11 \Rightarrow$ _____

11) $17 \leq -5 + x \Rightarrow$ _____

12) $x + 25 > 29 \Rightarrow x$_____

13) $x - 17 \geq 19 \Rightarrow$ _____

14) $x + 8 > -17 \Rightarrow$ _____

15) $x + 8 < -23 \Rightarrow$ _____

16) $16 \leq -5 + x \Rightarrow$ _____

17) $4x \leq 12 \Rightarrow$ _____

18) $28 \geq -7x \Rightarrow$ _____

19) $2x > -14 \Rightarrow$ _____

20) $13x \leq 39 \Rightarrow$ _____

21) $-8x > -16 \Rightarrow$ _____

22) $\frac{x}{2} < -6 \Rightarrow$ _____

23) $\frac{x}{6} > 6 \Rightarrow$ _____

24) $27 \leq \frac{x}{4} \Rightarrow$ _____

25) $\frac{x}{8} < -3 \Rightarrow$ _____

26) $6x \geq 18 \Rightarrow$ _____

27) $5x \geq -25 \Rightarrow$ _____

28) $3x > 45 \Rightarrow$ _____

29) $9x \leq 72 \Rightarrow$ _____

30) $-6x < -36 \Rightarrow$ _____

31) $70 > -10x \Rightarrow$ _____

Multi –Step Inequalities

✍ *Solve each inequality.*

1) $2x - 6 \leq 4 \rightarrow$ _____

2) $2 + 3x \geq 17 \rightarrow$ _____

3) $9 + 3x \geq 36 \rightarrow$ _____

4) $2x - 6 \leq 18 \rightarrow$ _____

5) $3x - 4 \leq 23 \rightarrow$ _____

6) $7x - 5 \leq 51 \rightarrow$ _____

7) $4x - 9 \leq 27 \rightarrow$ _____

8) $6x - 11 \leq 13 \rightarrow$ _____

9) $5x - 7 \leq 33 \rightarrow$ _____

10) $6 + 2x \geq 28 \rightarrow$ _____

11) $8 + 3x \geq 35 \rightarrow$ _____

12) $4 + 6x < 34 \rightarrow$ _____

13) $3 + 2x \geq 53 \rightarrow$ _____

14) $7 - 6x > 56 + x \rightarrow$ _____

15) $9 + 4x \geq 39 + 2x \rightarrow$ _____

16) $3 + 5x \geq 43 \rightarrow$ _____

17) $4 - 7x < 60 \rightarrow$ _____

18) $11 - 4x \geq 55 \rightarrow$ _____

19) $12 + x \geq 48 - 2x \rightarrow$ _____

20) $10 - 10x \leq -20 \rightarrow$ _____

21) $5 - 9x \geq -40 \rightarrow$ _____

22) $8 - 7x \geq 36 \rightarrow$ _____

23) $6 + 10x < 69 + 3x \rightarrow$ _____

24) $5 + 4x < 26 - 3x \rightarrow$ _____

25) $10 + 11x < 59 + 4x \rightarrow$ _____

26) $3 + 9x \geq 48 - 6x \rightarrow$ _____

Answers – Chapter 7

One–Step Equations

1) $x = 46$	9) $x = -27$	17) $x = 7$	25) $x = -12$
2) $x = 24$	10) $x = -10$	18) $x = -3$	26) $x = 56$
3) $x = 9$	11) $x = 22$	19) $x = -1$	27) $x = -6$
4) $x = 53$	12) $x = 9$	20) $x = 3$	28) $x = 7$
5) $x = 7$	13) $x = 32$	21) $x = -2$	29) $x = 6$
6) $x = 13$	14) $x = -26$	22) $x = -10$	30) $x = -5$
7) $x = -2$	15) $x = -27$	23) $x = 54$	31) $x = -6$
8) $x = -18$	16) $x = 25$	24) $x = 135$	

Multi –Step Equations

1) $x = 5$	9) $x = -8$	17) $x = 10$	25) $x = -4$
2) $x = -22$	10) $x = 15$	18) $x = -3$	26) $x = 1$
3) $x = 24$	11) $x = -4$	19) $x = -4$	27) $x = -5$
4) $x = -21$	12) $x = 4$	20) $x = 0$	28) $x = -8$
5) $x = -1$	13) $x = -13$	21) $x = -4$	29) $x = -4$
6) $x = 6$	14) $x = 1$	22) $x = -1$	30) $x = -5$
7) $x = -17$	15) $x = 9$	23) $x = -3$	31) $x = -2$
8) $x = -3$	16) $x = -1$	24) $x = -2$	32) $x = -19$

System of Equations

1) $x = 6, y = 1$

2) $x = -4 , y = -1$

3) $x = 42, y = -12$

4) $x = 2 , y = 1$

5) $x = -\frac{11}{2}, y = -5$

6) $x = 1 , y = -2$

7) $x = 1 , y = 2$

8) $x = 1 , y = 1$

9) $x = 3 , y = 2$

10) $x = 3 , y = -2$

11) $x = 1, y = 2$

12) $x = 2, y = -5$

13) $x = 1, y = 2$

14) $x = -5, y = 8$

15) $x = 3, y = 2$

16) $x = -3 , y = -4$

Graphing Single–Variable Inequalities

1) $x < 5$

2) $x \geq 2$

3) $x \geq -4$

4) $x \leq -1$

5) $x > -1$

6) $3 > x$

7) $2 \leq x$

8) $x > 0$

9) $-3 \leq x$

10) $-4 \leq x$

11) $x \leq 6$

12) $1 \leq x$

13) $-4 < x$

14) $x > -5$

One–Step Inequalities

1) $x < 29$

2) $20 \leq x$

3) $x > 40$

4) $x \geq 8$

5) $x > 41$

6) $x \geq -2$

7) $x < -2$

8) $x \leq -18$

9) $x \geq -27$

10) $x < -13$

11) $22 \leq x$

12) $x > 4$

13) $x \geq 36$

14) $x > -25$

15) $x < -31$

16) $21 \leq x$

17) $x \leq 3$

18) $-4 \leq x$

19) $x > -7$

20) $x \leq 3$

21) $x < 2$

22) $x < -12$

23) $x > 36$

24) $108 \leq x$

25) $x < -24$

26) $x \geq 3$

27) $x \geq -5$

28) $x > 15$

29) $x \leq 8$

30) $x > 6$

31) $-7 < x$

Multi –Step Inequalities

1) $x \leq 5$

2) $x \geq 5$

3) $x \geq 9$

4) $x \leq 12$

5) $x \leq 9$

6) $x \leq 8$

7) $x \leq 9$

8) $x \leq 4$

9) $x \leq 8$

10) $x \geq 11$

11) $x \geq 9$

12) $x < 5$

13) $x \geq 25$

14) $x < -7$

15) $x \geq 15$

16) $x \geq 8$

17) $x > -8$

18) $x \leq -11$

19) $x \geq 12$

20) $x \geq 3$

21) $x \leq 5$

22) $x \leq -4$

23) $x < 9$

24) $x < 3$

25) $x < 7$

26) $x \geq 3$

Chapter 8: Lines and Slope

Math Topics that you'll learn in this Chapter:

- ✓ Finding Slope
- ✓ Graphing Lines Using Slope–Intercept Form
- ✓ Writing Linear Equations
- ✓ Graphing Linear Inequalities
- ✓ Finding Midpoint
- ✓ Finding Distance of Two Points

Finding Slope

✎ *Find the slope of each line.*

1) $y = 2x - 8$, Slope $=$

2) $y = -6x + 3$, Slope $=$

3) $y = -x - 5$, Slope $=$

4) $y = -2x - 9$, Slope $=$

5) $y = 5 + 2x$, Slope $=$

6) $y = 1 - 8x$, Slope $=$

7) $y = -4x + 3$, Slope $=$

8) $y = -9x + 8$, Slope $=$

9) $y = -2x + 4$, Slope $=$

10) $y = 9x - 8$, Slope $=$

11) $y = \frac{1}{2}x + 4$, Slope $=$

12) $y = -\frac{2}{5}x + 7$, Slope $=$

13) $-x + 3y = 5$, Slope $=$

14) $4x + 4y = 6$, Slope $=$

15) $6y - 2x = 10$, Slope $=$

16) $3y - x = 2$, Slope $=$

✎ *Find the slope of the line through each pair of points.*

17) $(4, 4), (8, 12)$, Slope $=$

23) $(8, 4), (9, 6)$, Slope $=$

18) $(-2, 4), (0, 6)$, Slope $=$

24) $(10, -1), (7, 8)$, Slope $=$

19) $(6, -2), (2, 6)$, Slope $=$

25) $(16, -3), (13, -6)$, Slope $=$

20) $(-4, -2), (0, 6)$, Slope $=$

26) $(12,5), (8, 1)$, Slope $=$

21) $(6, 2), (3, 5)$, Slope $=$

27) $(6, 6), (8, 10)$, Slope $=$

22) $(-5,1), (-1, 9)$, Slope $=$

28) $(10, -1), (8, 1)$, Slope $=$

Graphing Lines Using Slope–Intercept Form

✎ *Sketch the graph of each line.*

1) $y = -x + 1$

2) $y = 2x - 4$

3) $y = -x + 6$

4) $y = x - 4$

5) $y = 2x - 2$

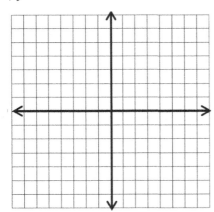

6) $y = -\frac{1}{2}x + 2$

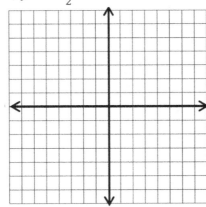

Writing Linear Equations

✎ **Write the equation of the line through the given points.**

1) through: $(2, -2), (3, 4)$ $y =$

2) through: $(-2, 4), (1, 7)$ $y =$

3) through: $(-1, 3), (3, 7)$ $y =$

4) through: $(6, 5), (3, 2)$ $y =$

5) through: $(7, -10), (2, 10)$ $y =$

6) through: $(7, 2), (6, 1)$ $y =$

7) through: $(6, -1), (4, 1)$ $y =$

8) through: $(-2, 8), (-4, -6)$ $y =$

9) through: $(-2, 5), (-3, 4)$ $y =$

10) through: $(6, 8), (8, -6)$ $y =$

11) through: $(-2, 5), (-4, -3)$ $y =$

12) through: $(8, 8), (4, -8)$ $y =$

13) through: $(7, -4)$, Slope: -1 $y =$

14) through: $(4, -10)$, Slope: -2 $y =$

15) through: $(6, 10)$, Slope: 9 $y =$

16) through: $(-6, 8)$, Slope: -2 $y =$

✎ **Solve each problem.**

17) What is the equation of a line with slope 6 and intercept 4? _____

18) What is the equation of a line with slope 5 and intercept 9? _____

19) What is the equation of a line with slope 8 and passes through point $(2, 8)$?

_____

20) What is the equation of a line with slope -3 and passes through point $(-4, 10)$? _____

Finding Midpoint

✒ *Find the midpoint of the line segment with the given endpoints.*

1) $(4, 4), (0, 4),$ $midpoint = (\underline{}, \underline{})$

2) $(5, 1), (-1, 5),$ $midpoint = (\underline{}, \underline{})$

3) $(4, -2), (0, 6),$ $midpoint = (\underline{}, \underline{})$

4) $(-3, 3), (-1, 5),$ $midpoint = (\underline{}, \underline{})$

5) $(5, -2), (9, -6),$ $midpoint = (\underline{}, \underline{})$

6) $(-6, -3), (4, -7),$ $midpoint = (\underline{}, \underline{})$

7) $(7, 0), (-7, 8),$ $midpoint = (\underline{}, \underline{})$

8) $(-8, 4), (-4, 0),$ $midpoint = (\underline{}, \underline{})$

9) $(-3, 6), (9, -8),$ $midpoint = (\underline{}, \underline{})$

10) $(6, 8), (6, -6),$ $midpoint = (\underline{}, \underline{})$

11) $(6, 7), (-8, 5),$ $midpoint = (\underline{}, \underline{})$

12) $(9, 3), (-3, -9),$ $midpoint = (\underline{}, \underline{})$

13) $(-6, 12), (-4, 6),$ $midpoint = (\underline{}, \underline{})$

14) $(10, 7), (8, -3),$ $midpoint = (\underline{}, \underline{})$

15) $(13, 7), (-5, 3),$ $midpoint = (\underline{}, \underline{})$

16) $(-9, -4), (-5, 8),$ $midpoint = (\underline{}, \underline{})$

17) $(12, 5), (6, 15),$ $midpoint = (\underline{}, \underline{})$

18) $(-6, -10), (12, -2),$ $midpoint = (\underline{}, \underline{})$

19) $(14, 13), (-4, 9),$ $midpoint = (\underline{}, \underline{})$

20) $(10, -4), (8, 12),$ $midpoint = (\underline{}, \underline{})$

Finding Distance of Two Points

✎ *Find the distance of each pair of points.*

1) $(0, 9), (4, 6),$

    Distance = ____

2) $(-4, 6), (8, 11),$

    Distance = ____

3) $(-6, 1), (-3, 5),$

    Distance = ____

4) $(-3, 2), (3, 10),$

    Distance = ____

5) $(-5, 3), (4, -9),$

    Distance = ____

6) $(-7, -5), (5, 0),$

    Distance = ____

7) $(4, 3), (-4, -12),$

    Distance = ____

8) $(10, 1), (-5, -19),$

    Distance = ____

9) $(3, 3), (-1, 5),$

    Distance = ____

10) $(2, -1), (10, 5),$

    Distance = ____

11) $(-3, 7), (-1, 4),$

    Distance = ____

12) $(5, -2), (9, -5),$

    Distance = ____

13) $(-8, 4), (4, 9),$

    Distance = ____

14) $(6, 8), (6, -6),$

    Distance = ____

15) $(6, -6), (0, 2),$

    Distance = ____

16) $(-4, 10), (-4, 4),$

    Distance = ____

17) $(-7, -6), (-2, 6),$

    Distance = ____

18) $(11, 0), (3, 15),$

    Distance = ____

Answers – Chapter 8

Finding Slope

1) 2	7) −4	13) $\frac{1}{3}$	18) 1	24) −3
2) −6	8) −9	14) −1	19) −2	25) 1
3) −1	9) −2	15) $\frac{1}{3}$	20) 2	26) 1
4) −2	10) 9	16) $\frac{1}{3}$	21) −1	27) 2
5) 2	11) $\frac{1}{2}$	17) 2	22) 2	28) −1
6) −8	12) $-\frac{2}{5}$		23) 2	

Graphing Lines Using Slope–Intercept Form

1) $y = -x + 1$

2) $y = 2x - 4$

3) $y = -x + 6$

4) $y = x - 4$

5) $y = 2x - 2$

6) $y = -\frac{1}{2}x + 2$

Writing Linear Equations

1) $y = 6x - 14$

2) $y = x + 6$

3) $y = x + 4$

4) $y = x - 1$

5) $y = -4x + 18$

6) $y = x - 5$

7) $y = -x + 5$

8) $y = 7x + 22$

9) $y = x + 7$

10) $y = -7x + 50$

11) $y = 4x + 13$

12) $y = 4x - 24$

13) $y = -x + 3$

14) $y = -2x - 2$

15) $y = 9x - 44$

16) $y = -2x - 4$

17) $y = 6x + 4$

18) $y = 5x + 9$

19) $y = 8x - 8$

20) $y = -3x - 2$

Finding Midpoint

1) $midpoint = (2, 4)$

2) $midpoint = (2, 3)$

3) $midpoint = (2, 2)$

4) $midpoint = (-2, 4)$

5) $midpoint = (7, -4)$

6) $midpoint = (-1, -5)$

7) $midpoint = (0, 4)$

8) $midpoint = (-6, 2)$

9) $midpoint = (3, -1)$

10) $midpoint = (6, 1)$

11) $midpoint = (-1, 6)$

12) $midpoint = (3, -3)$

13) $midpoint = (-5, 9)$

14) $midpoint = (9, 2)$

15) $midpoint = (4, 5)$

16) $midpoint = (-7, 2)$

17) $midpoint = (9, 10)$

18) $midpoint = (3, -6)$

19) $midpoint = (5, 11)$

20) $midpoint = (9, 4)$

Finding Distance of Two Points

1) Distance $= 5$

2) Distance $= 13$

3) Distance $= 5$

4) Distance $= 10$

5) Distance $= 15$

6) Distance $= 13$

7) Distance $= 17$

8) Distance $= 25$

9) Distance $= \sqrt{20} = 2\sqrt{5}$

10) Distance $= 10$

11) Distance $= \sqrt{13}$

12) Distance $= 5$

13) Distance $= 13$

14) Distance $= 14$

15) Distance $= 10$

16) Distance $= 6$

17) Distance $= 13$

18) Distance $= 17$

Chapter 9: Exponents and Variables

Math Topics that you'll learn in this Chapter:

- ✓ Multiplication Property of Exponents
- ✓ Division Property of Exponents
- ✓ Powers of Products and Quotients
- ✓ Zero and Negative Exponents
- ✓ Negative Exponents and Negative Bases
- ✓ Scientific Notation
- ✓ Radicals

Multiplication Property of Exponents

✎ *Simplify and write the answer in exponential form.*

1) $3 \times 3^2 =$

2) $4^3 \times 4 =$

3) $2^2 \times 2^2 =$

4) $6^2 \times 6^2 =$

5) $7^3 \times 7^2 \times 7 =$

6) $2 \times 2^2 \times 2^2 =$

7) $5^3 \times 5^2 \times 5 \times 5 =$

8) $2x \times x =$

9) $x^3 \times x^2 =$

10) $x^4 \times x^4 =$

11) $x^2 \times x^2 \times x^2 =$

12) $6x \times 6x =$

13) $2x^2 \times 2x^2 =$

14) $3x^2 \times x =$

15) $4x^4 \times 4x^4 \times 4x^4 =$

16) $2x^2 \times x^2 =$

17) $x^4 \times 3x =$

18) $x \times 2x^2 =$

19) $5x^4 \times 5x^4 =$

20) $2yx^2 \times 2x =$

21) $3x^4 \times y^2x^4 =$

22) $y^2x^3 \times y^5x^2 =$

23) $4yx^3 \times 2x^2y^3 =$

24) $6x^2 \times 6x^3y^4 =$

25) $3x^4y^5 \times 7x^2y^3 =$

26) $7x^2y^5 \times 9xy^3 =$

27) $7xy^4 \times 4x^3y^3 =$

28) $3x^5y^3 \times 8x^2y^3 =$

29) $6x \times y^5x^2 \times y^3 =$

30) $yx^3 \times 3y^3x^2 \times 2xy =$

31) $5yx^3 \times 4y^2x \times xy^3 =$

32) $6x^2 \times 3x^3y^4 \times 10yx^3 =$

Division Property of Exponents

✏️ *Simplify and write the answer.*

1) $\dfrac{3^2}{3^3} =$

2) $\dfrac{2^6}{2^2} =$

3) $\dfrac{4^4}{4} =$

4) $\dfrac{5}{5^4} =$

5) $\dfrac{x}{x^3} =$

6) $\dfrac{3 \times 3^3}{3^2 \times 3^4} =$

7) $\dfrac{5^8}{5^3} =$

8) $\dfrac{5 \times 5^6}{5^2 \times 5^7} =$

9) $\dfrac{3^4 \times 3^7}{3^2 \times 3^8} =$

10) $\dfrac{5x}{10x^3} =$

11) $\dfrac{5x^3}{2x^5} =$

12) $\dfrac{18x^3}{14x^6} =$

13) $\dfrac{12x^3}{8xy^8} =$

14) $\dfrac{24xy^3}{4x^4y^2} =$

15) $\dfrac{21x^3y^9}{7xy^5} =$

16) $\dfrac{36x^2y^9}{4x^3} =$

17) $\dfrac{18x^3y^4}{10x^6y^8} =$

18) $\dfrac{16y^2x^{14}}{24yx^8} =$

19) $\dfrac{15x^4y}{9x^9y^2} =$

20) $\dfrac{7x^7y^2}{28x^5y^6} =$

Powers of Products and Quotients

✎ *Simplify and write the answer.*

1) $(3^2)^2 =$

2) $(5^2)^3 =$

3) $(3 \times 3^3)^4 =$

4) $(6 \times 6^4)^2 =$

5) $(3^3 \times 3^2)^3 =$

6) $(5^4 \times 5^5)^2 =$

7) $(2 \times 2^4)^2 =$

8) $(2x^6)^2 =$

9) $(11x^5)^2 =$

10) $(4x^2y^4)^4 =$

11) $(2x^4y^4)^3 =$

12) $(3x^2y^2)^2 =$

13) $(3x^4y^3)^4 =$

14) $(2x^6y^8)^2 =$

15) $(12x^3x)^3 =$

16) $(5x^9x^6)^3 =$

17) $(5x^{10}y^3)^3 =$

18) $(14x^3x^3)^2 =$

19) $(3x^3 5x)^2 =$

20) $(10x^{11}y^3)^2 =$

21) $(9x^7y^5)^2 =$

22) $(4x^4y^6)^5 =$

23) $(3x4y^3)^2 =$

24) $\left(\frac{6x}{x^2}\right)^2 =$

25) $\left(\frac{x^5y^5}{x^2y^2}\right)^3 =$

26) $\left(\frac{24x}{4x^6}\right)^2 =$

27) $\left(\frac{x^5}{x^6y^2}\right)^2 =$

28) $\left(\frac{xy^3}{x^2y^5}\right)^3 =$

29) $\left(\frac{3xy^3}{x^4}\right)^2 =$

30) $\left(\frac{xy^5}{4xy^3}\right)^3 =$

Chapter 9: Exponents and Variables

Zero and Negative Exponents

✎ *Evaluate the following expressions.*

1) $2^{-1} =$

2) $3^{-2} =$

3) $0^{10} =$

4) $1^{-8} =$

5) $8^{-1} =$

6) $8^{-2} =$

7) $2^{-4} =$

8) $10^{-2} =$

9) $9^{-2} =$

10) $3^{-3} =$

11) $7^{-3} =$

12) $3^{-4} =$

13) $6^{-3} =$

14) $5^{-3} =$

15) $22^{-1} =$

16) $4^{-4} =$

17) $5^{-4} =$

18) $15^{-2} =$

19) $4^{-5} =$

20) $9^{-3} =$

21) $3^{-5} =$

22) $5^{-4} =$

23) $12^{-2} =$

24) $15^{-3} =$

25) $20^{-3} =$

26) $50^{-2} =$

27) $18^{-3} =$

28) $24^{-2} =$

29) $30^{-3} =$

30) $10^{-5} =$

31) $\left(\frac{1}{8}\right)^{-1} =$

32) $\left(\frac{1}{5}\right)^{-2} =$

33) $\left(\frac{1}{7}\right)^{-2} =$

34) $\left(\frac{2}{3}\right)^{-2} =$

35) $\left(\frac{1}{5}\right)^{-3} =$

36) $\left(\frac{3}{4}\right)^{-2} =$

37) $\left(\frac{2}{5}\right)^{-2} =$

38) $\left(\frac{1}{2}\right)^{-8} =$

39) $\left(\frac{2}{3}\right)^{-3} =$

40) $\left(\frac{3}{4}\right)^{-3} =$

41) $\left(\frac{5}{6}\right)^{-2} =$

42) $\left(\frac{6}{9}\right)^{-2} =$

Negative Exponents and Negative Bases

✎ *Simplify and write the answer.*

1) $-2^{-1} =$

2) $-4^{-2} =$

3) $-3^{-4} =$

4) $-x^{-5} =$

5) $2x^{-1} =$

6) $-4x^{-3} =$

7) $-12x^{-5} =$

8) $-5x^{-2}y^{-3} =$

9) $20x^{-4}y^{-1} =$

10) $14a^{-6}b^{-7} =$

11) $-12x^2y^{-3} =$

12) $-\frac{25}{x^{-6}} =$

13) $-\frac{2x}{a^{-4}} =$

14) $\left(-\frac{1}{3x}\right)^{-2} =$

15) $\left(-\frac{3}{4x}\right)^{-2} =$

16) $-\frac{9}{a^{-7}b^{-2}} =$

17) $-\frac{5x}{x^{-3}} =$

18) $-\frac{a^{-3}}{b^{-2}} =$

19) $-\frac{8}{x^{-3}} =$

20) $\frac{5b}{-9c^{-4}} =$

21) $\frac{9ab}{a^{-3}b^{-1}} =$

22) $-\frac{15a^{-2}}{30b^{-3}} =$

23) $\frac{4ab^{-2}}{-3c^{-2}} =$

24) $\left(\frac{3a}{2c}\right)^{-2} =$

25) $\left(-\frac{3x}{4yz}\right)^{-2} =$

26) $\frac{15ab^{-6}}{-9c^{-2}} =$

27) $\left(-\frac{x^3}{x^4}\right)^{-3} =$

28) $\left(-\frac{x^{-2}}{2x^2}\right)^{-2} =$

Scientific Notation

✎ *Write each number in scientific notation.*

1) $0.114 =$

2) $0.06 =$

3) $8.6 =$

4) $30 =$

5) $60 =$

6) $0.004 =$

7) $78 =$

8) $1,600 =$

9) $1,450 =$

10) $31,000 =$

11) $2,000,000 =$

12) $0.0000003 =$

13) $554,000 =$

14) $0.000725 =$

15) $0.00034 =$

16) $86,000,000 =$

17) $62,000 =$

18) $97,000,000 =$

19) $0.0000045 =$

20) $0.0019 =$

✎ *Write each number in standard notation.*

21) $2 \times 10^{-1} =$

22) $8 \times 10^{-2} =$

23) $1.8 \times 10^3 =$

24) $9 \times 10^{-4} =$

25) $1.7 \times 10^{-2} =$

26) $9 \times 10^3 =$

27) $6 \times 10^4 =$

28) $2.18 \times 10^5 =$

29) $5 \times 10^{-3} =$

30) $9.4 \times 10^{-5} =$

Radicals

✏️ *Simplify and write the answer.*

1) $\sqrt{1} = $ ____

2) $\sqrt{0} = $ ____

3) $\sqrt{16} = $ ____

4) $\sqrt{4} = $ ____

5) $\sqrt{9} = $ ____

6) $\sqrt{25} = $ ____

7) $\sqrt{49} = $ ____

8) $\sqrt{36} = $ ____

9) $\sqrt{64} = $ ____

10) $\sqrt{81} = $ ____

11) $\sqrt{121} = $ ____

12) $\sqrt{225} = $ ____

13) $\sqrt{144} = $ ____

14) $\sqrt{100} = $ ____

15) $\sqrt{256} = $ ____

16) $\sqrt{289} = $ ____

17) $\sqrt{324} = $ ____

18) $\sqrt{400} = $ ____

19) $\sqrt{900} = $ ____

20) $\sqrt{529} = $ ____

21) $\sqrt{361} = $ ____

22) $\sqrt{169} = $ ____

23) $\sqrt{196} = $ ____

24) $\sqrt{90} = $ ____

✏️ *Evaluate.*

25) $\sqrt{6} \times \sqrt{6} = $

26) $\sqrt{5} \times \sqrt{5} = $

27) $\sqrt{8} \times \sqrt{8} = $

28) $\sqrt{2} + \sqrt{2} = $

29) $\sqrt{8} + \sqrt{8} = $

30) $6\sqrt{5} - 2\sqrt{5} = $

31) $\sqrt{25} \times \sqrt{16} = $

32) $\sqrt{25} \times \sqrt{64} = $

33) $\sqrt{64} \times \sqrt{49} = $

34) $5\sqrt{5} \times 3\sqrt{5} = $

35) $7\sqrt{3} \times 2\sqrt{3} = $

36) $5\sqrt{2} - \sqrt{8} = $

Answers – Chapter 9

Multiplication Property of Exponents

1) 3^3

2) 4^4

3) 2^4

4) 6^4

5) 7^6

6) 2^5

7) 5^7

8) $2x^2$

9) x^5

10) x^8

11) x^6

12) $36x^2$

13) $4x^4$

14) $3x^3$

15) $64x^{12}$

16) $2x^4$

17) $3x^5$

18) $2x^3$

19) $25x^8$

20) $4x^3y$

21) $3x^8y^2$

22) x^5y^7

23) $8x^5y^4$

24) $36x^5y^4$

25) $21x^6y^8$

26) $63x^3y^8$

27) $28x^4y^7$

28) $24x^7y^6$

29) $6x^3y^8$

30) $6x^6y^5$

31) $20x^5y^6$

32) $180x^8y^5$

Division Property of Exponents

1) $\frac{1}{3}$

2) 2^4

3) 4^3

4) $\frac{1}{5^3}$

5) $\frac{1}{x^2}$

6) $\frac{1}{3^2}$

7) 5^5

8) $\frac{1}{5^2}$

9) 3

10) $\frac{1}{2x^2}$

11) $\frac{5}{2x^2}$

12) $\frac{9}{7x^3}$

13) $\frac{3x^2}{2y^8}$

14) $\frac{6y}{x^3}$

15) $3x^2y^4$

16) $\frac{9y^9}{x}$

17) $\frac{9}{5x^3y^4}$

18) $\frac{2yx^6}{3}$

19) $\frac{5}{3x^5y}$

20) $\frac{x^2}{4y^4}$

Powers of Products and Quotients

1) 3^4

2) 5^6

3) 3^{16}

4) 6^{10}

5) 3^{15}

6) 5^{18}

7) 2^{10}

8) $4x^{12}$

9) $121x^{10}$

10) $256x^8y^{16}$

11) $8x^{12}y^{12}$

12) $9x^4y^4$

13) $81x^{16}y^{12}$

14) $4x^{12}y^{16}$

15) $1,728x^{12}$

16) $125x^{45}$

17) $125x^{30}y^9$

18) $196x^{12}$

19) $225x^8$

20) $100x^{22}y^6$

21) $81x^{14}y^{10}$

22) $1,024x^{20}y^{30}$

23) $144x^2y^6$

24) $\dfrac{36}{x^2}$

25) x^9y^9

26) $\dfrac{36}{x^{10}}$

27) $\dfrac{1}{x^2y^4}$

28) $\dfrac{1}{x^3y^6}$

29) $\dfrac{9y^6}{x^6}$

30) $\dfrac{y^6}{64}$

Zero and Negative Exponents

1) $\frac{1}{2}$

2) $\frac{1}{9}$

3) 0

4) 1

5) $\frac{1}{8}$

6) $\frac{1}{64}$

7) $\frac{1}{16}$

8) $\frac{1}{100}$

9) $\frac{1}{81}$

10) $\frac{1}{27}$

11) $\frac{1}{343}$

12) $\frac{1}{81}$

13) $\frac{1}{216}$

14) $\frac{1}{125}$

15) $\frac{1}{22}$

16) $\frac{1}{256}$

17) $\frac{1}{625}$

18) $\frac{1}{225}$

19) $\frac{1}{1,024}$

20) $\frac{1}{729}$

21) $\frac{1}{243}$

22) $\frac{1}{625}$

23) $\frac{1}{144}$

24) $\frac{1}{3,375}$

25) $\frac{1}{8,000}$

26) $\frac{1}{2,500}$

27) $\frac{1}{5,832}$

28) $\frac{1}{576}$

29) $\frac{1}{27,000}$

30) $\frac{1}{100,000}$

31) 8

32) 25

33) 49

34) $\frac{9}{4}$

35) 125

36) $\frac{16}{9}$

37) $\frac{25}{4}$

38) 256

39) $\frac{27}{8}$

40) $\frac{64}{27}$

41) $\frac{36}{25}$

42) $\frac{81}{36}$

Negative Exponents and Negative Bases

1) $-\dfrac{1}{2}$

2) $-\dfrac{1}{16}$

3) $-\dfrac{1}{81}$

4) $-\dfrac{1}{x^5}$

5) $\dfrac{2}{x}$

6) $-\dfrac{4}{x^3}$

7) $-\dfrac{12}{x^5}$

8) $-\dfrac{5}{x^2 y^3}$

9) $\dfrac{20}{x^4 y}$

10) $\dfrac{14}{a^6 b^7}$

11) $-\dfrac{12x^2}{y^3}$

12) $-25x^6$

13) $-2xa^4$

14) $9x^2$

15) $\dfrac{16x^2}{9}$

16) $-9a^7 b^2$

17) $-5x^4$

18) $-\dfrac{b^2}{a^3}$

19) $-8x^3$

20) $-\dfrac{5bc^4}{9}$

21) $9a^4 b^2$

22) $-\dfrac{b^3}{2a^2}$

23) $-\dfrac{4ac^2}{3b^2}$

24) $\dfrac{4c^2}{9a^2}$

25) $\dfrac{16y^2 z^2}{9x^2}$

26) $-\dfrac{5ac^2}{3b^6}$

27) $-x^3$

28) $4x^8$

Scientific Notation

1) 1.14×10^{-1}

2) 6×10^{-2}

3) 8.6×10^{0}

4) 3×10^{1}

5) 6×10^{1}

6) 4×10^{-3}

7) 7.8×10^{1}

8) 1.6×10^{3}

9) 1.45×10^{3}

10) 3.1×10^{4}

11) 2×10^{6}

12) 3×10^{-7}

13) 5.54×10^{5}

14) 7.25×10^{-4}

15) 3.4×10^{-4}

16) 8.6×10^{7}

17) 6.2×10^{4}

18) 9.7×10^{7}

19) 4.5×10^{-6}

20) 1.9×10^{-3}

21) 0.2

22) 0.08

23) $1,800$

24) 0.0009

25) 0.017

26) $9,000$

27) $60,000$

28) $218,000$

29) 0.005

30) 0.000094

Radicals

1) 1

2) 0

3) 4

4) 2

5) 3

6) 5

7) 7

8) 6

9) 8

10) 9

11) 11

12) 15

13) 12

14) 10

15) 16

16) 17

17) 18

18) 20

19) 30

20) 23

21) 19

22) 13

23) 14

24) $3\sqrt{10}$

25) 6

26) 5

27) 8

28) $2\sqrt{2}$

29) $2\sqrt{8} = 4\sqrt{2}$

30) $4\sqrt{5}$

31) 20

32) 40

33) 56

34) 75

35) 42

36) $3\sqrt{2}$

Chapter 10:
Polynomials

Math Topics that you'll learn in this Chapter:

- ✓ Simplifying Polynomials
- ✓ Adding and Subtracting Polynomials
- ✓ Multiplying Monomials
- ✓ Multiplying and Dividing Monomials
- ✓ Multiplying a Polynomial and a Monomial
- ✓ Multiplying Binomials
- ✓ Factoring Trinomials

Chapter 10: Polynomials

Simplifying Polynomials

✎ *Simplify each expression.*

1) $3(2x + 1) = $ _____

2) $2(4x - 6) = $ _____

3) $4(3x + 3) = $ _____

4) $2(4x + 5) = $ _____

5) $-3(8x - 7) = $ _____

6) $2x(3x + 4) = $ _____

7) $3x^2 + 3x^2 - 2x^3 = $ _____

8) $2x - x^2 + 6x^3 + 4 = $ _____

9) $5x + 2x^2 - 9x^3 = $ _____

10) $7x^2 + 5x^4 - 2x^3 = $ _____

11) $-3x^2 + 5x^3 + 6x^4 = $ _____

12) $(x - 3)(x - 4) = $ _____

13) $(x - 5)(x + 4) = $ _____

14) $(x - 6)(x - 3) = $ _____

15) $(2x + 5)(x + 8) = $ _____

16) $(3x - 8)(x + 4) = $ _____

17) $-8x^2 + 2x^3 - 10x^4 + 5x = $ _____

18) $11 - 6x^2 + 5x^2 - 12x^3 + 22 = $ _____

19) $3x^2 - 4x + 4x^3 + 10x - 21x = $ _____

20) $10 - 6x^2 + 5x^2 - 3x^3 + 2 = $ _____

21) $3x^5 - 2x^3 + 8x^2 - x^5 = $ _____

22) $(5x^3 - 1) + (4x^3 - 6x^3) = $ _____

Chapter 10: Polynomials

Adding and Subtracting Polynomials

✍ *Add or subtract expressions.*

1) $(x^2 - 5) + (x^2 + 6) =$ _____

2) $(2x^2 - 6) - (3 - 2x^2) =$ _____

3) $(x^3 + 3x^2) - (x^3 + 6) =$ _____

4) $(4x^3 - x^2) + (6x^2 - 8x) =$ _____

5) $(2x^3 + 3x) - (5x^3 + 2) =$ _____

6) $(5x^3 - 2) + (2x^3 + 10) =$ _____

7) $(7x^3 + 5) - (9 - 4x^3) =$ _____

8) $(5x^2 + 3x^3) - (2x^3 + 6) =$ _____

9) $(8x^2 - x) + (4x - 8x^2) =$ _____

10) $(6x + 9x^2) - (5x + 2) =$ _____

11) $(7x^4 - 2x) - (6x - 2x^4) =$ _____

12) $(2x - 4x^3) - (9x^3 + 6x) =$ _____

13) $(8x^3 - 8x^2) - (6x^2 - 3x) =$ _____

14) $(9x^2 - 6) + (5x^2 - 4x^3) =$ _____

15) $(8x^3 + 3x^4) - (x^4 - 3x^3) =$ _____

16) $(-4x^3 - 2x) + (5x - 2x^3) =$ _____

17) $(9x - 5x^4) - (8x^4 + 4x) =$ _____

18) $(8x - 3x^2) - (7x^4 - 3x^2) =$ _____

19) $(9x^3 - 7) + (5x^3 - 4x^2) =$ _____

20) $(7x^3 + x^4) - (6x^4 - 5x^3) =$ _____

Multiplying Monomials

✎ *Simplify each expression.*

1) $4x^7 \times x^3 =$

2) $6y^2 \times 6y^3 =$

3) $-6z^7 \times 4z^4 =$

4) $5x^5y \times 8xy^3 =$

5) $-6xy^8 \times 3x^5y^3 =$

6) $7a^4b^2 \times 3a^8b =$

7) $5xy^5 \times 3x^3y^4 =$

8) $5p^5q^4 \times (-6pq^4) =$

9) $8s^6t^2 \times 6s^3t^7 =$

10) $(-8x^5y^2) \times 4x^6y^3 =$

11) $9xy^6z \times 3y^4z^2 =$

12) $12x^5y^4 \times 2x^8y =$

13) $4pq^5 \times (-7p^4q^8) =$

14) $9s^4t^2 \times (-5st^5) =$

15) $10p^3q^5 \times (-4p^4q^6) =$

16) $(-5p^2q^4r) \times 7pq^5r^3 =$

17) $(-9a^4b^7c^4) \times (-4a^7b) =$

18) $7u^5v^9 \times (-5u^{12}v^7) =$

19) $4u^4v^9z^2 \times (-5uv^8z) =$

20) $(-6xy^3z^5) \times 3x^3yz^7 =$

21) $6x^2y^3z^5 \times (-7x^4y^2z) =$

22) $7a^5b^8c^{12} \times 4a^6b^5c^9 =$

Multiplying and Dividing Monomials

✍ *Simplify each expression.*

1) $(3x^5)(2x^2) =$

_____

2) $(6x^5)(2x^4) =$

_____

3) $(-7x^9)(2x^5) =$

_____

4) $(7x^7y^9)(-5x^6y^6) =$

_____

5) $(8x^5y^6)(3x^2y^5) =$

_____

6) $(8yx^2)(7y^5x^3) =$

_____

7) $(4x^2y)(2x^2y^3) =$

_____

8) $(-2x^9y^4)(-9x^6y^8) =$

_____

9) $(-5x^8y^2)(-6x^4y^5) =$

_____

10) $(8x^8y)(-7x^4y^3) =$

_____

11) $(9x^6y^2)(6x^7y^4) =$

12) $(8x^9y^5)(6x^5y^4) =$

_____

13) $(-5x^8y^9)(7x^7y^8) =$

_____

14) $(6x^2y^5)(5x^3y^2) =$

_____

15) $(9x^5y^{12})(4x^7y^9) =$

_____

16) $(-10x^{14}y^8)(2x^7y^5) =$

_____

17) $\frac{6x^5y^7}{xy^6} =$

_____

18) $\frac{9x^6y^6}{3x^4y} =$

_____

19) $\frac{16x^4y^6}{4xy} =$

_____

20) $\frac{-30x^9y^8}{5x^5y^4} =$

_____

Multiplying a Polynomial and a Monomial

✎ *Find each product.*

1) $x(x - 5) =$

_____

2) $2(3 + x) =$

_____

3) $x(x - 7) =$

_____

4) $x(x + 9) =$

_____

5) $2x(x - 2) =$

_____

6) $5(4x + 3) =$

_____

7) $4x(3x - 4) =$

_____

8) $x(5x + 2y) =$

_____

9) $3x(x - 2y) =$

_____

10) $6x(3x - 4y) =$

_____

11) $2x(3x - 8) =$

_____

12) $6x(4x - 6y) =$

_____

13) $3x(4x - 2y) =$

_____

14) $2x(2x - 6y) =$

_____

15) $5x(x^2 + y^2) =$

_____

16) $3x(2x^2 - y^2) =$

_____

17) $6(9x^2 + 3y^2) =$

_____

18) $4x(-3x^2y + 2y) =$

_____

19) $-3(6x^2 - 5xy + 3) =$

_____

20) $6(x^2 - 4xy - 3) =$

_____

Multiplying Binomials

✎ *Find each product.*

1) $(x - 3)(x + 4) =$

_____

2) $(x + 3)(x + 5) =$

_____

3) $(x - 6)(x - 7) =$

_____

4) $(x - 9)(x - 4) =$

_____

5) $(x - 7)(x - 5) =$

_____

6) $(x + 6)(x + 2) =$

_____

7) $(x - 9)(x + 3) =$

_____

8) $(x - 8)(x - 5) =$

_____

9) $(x + 3)(x + 7) =$

_____

10) $(x - 9)(x + 4) =$

_____

11) $(x + 6)(x + 6) =$

_____

12) $(x + 7)(x + 7) =$

_____

13) $(x - 8)(x + 7) =$

_____

14) $(x + 9)(x + 9) =$

_____

15) $(x - 8)(x - 8) =$

_____

16) $(x - 9)(x + 5) =$

_____

17) $(2x - 5)(x + 4) =$

_____

18) $(2x + 6)(x + 3) =$

_____

19) $(2x + 4)(x + 5) =$

_____

20) $(2x - 3)(2x + 2) =$

_____

Factoring Trinomials

✏️ *Factor each trinomial.*

1) $x^2 + 5x + 4 =$

_____

2) $x^2 + 5x + 6 =$

_____

3) $x^2 - 4x + 3 =$

_____

4) $x^2 - 10x + 25 =$

_____

5) $x^2 - 13x + 40 =$

_____

6) $x^2 + 8x + 12 =$

_____

7) $x^2 - 6x - 27 =$

_____

8) $x^2 - 14x + 48 =$

_____

9) $x^2 + 15x + 56 =$

_____

10) $x^2 - 5x - 36 =$

_____

11) $x^2 + 12x + 36 =$

_____

12) $x^2 + 16x + 63 =$

_____

13) $x^2 + x - 72 =$

_____

14) $x^2 + 18x + 81 =$

_____

15) $x^2 - 16x + 64 =$

_____

16) $x^2 - 18x + 81 =$

_____

17) $2x^2 + 10x + 8 =$

_____

18) $2x^2 + 4x - 6 =$

_____

19) $2x^2 + 9x + 4 =$

_____

20) $4x^2 + 4x - 24 =$

_____

Answers – Chapter 10

Simplifying Polynomials

1) $6x + 3$

2) $8x - 12$

3) $12x + 12$

4) $8x + 10$

5) $-24x + 21$

6) $6x^2 + 8x$

7) $-2x^3 + 6x^2$

8) $6x^3 - x^2 + 2x + 4$

9) $-9x^3 + 2x^2 + 5x$

10) $5x^4 - 2x^3 + 7x^2$

11) $6x^4 + 5x^3 - 3x^2$

12) $x^2 - 7x + 12$

13) $x^2 - x - 20$

14) $x^2 - 9x + 18$

15) $2x^2 + 21x + 40$

16) $3x^2 + 4x - 32$

17) $-10x^4 + 2x^3 - 8x^2 + 5x$

18) $-12x^3 - x^2 + 33$

19) $4x^3 + 3x^2 - 15x$

20) $-3x^3 - x^2 + 12$

21) $2x^5 - 2x^3 + 8x^2$

22) $3x^3 - 1$

Adding and Subtracting Polynomials

1) $2x^2 + 1$

2) $4x^2 - 9$

3) $3x^2 - 6$

4) $4x^3 + 5x^2 - 8x$

5) $-3x^3 + 3x - 2$

6) $7x^3 + 8$

7) $11x^3 - 4$

8) $x^3 + 5x^2 - 6$

9) $3x$

10) $9x^2 + x - 2$

11) $9x^4 - 8x$

12) $-13x^3 - 4x$

13) $8x^3 - 14x^2 + 3x$

14) $-4x^3 + 14x^2 - 6$

15) $2x^4 + 11x^3$

16) $-6x^3 + 3x$

17) $-13x^4 + 5x$

18) $-7x^4 + 8x$

19) $14x^3 - 4x^2 - 7$

20) $-5x^4 + 12x^3$

Multiplying Monomials

1) $4x^{10}$

2) $36y^5$

3) $-24z^{11}$

4) $40x^6y^4$

5) $-18x^6y^{11}$

6) $21a^{12}b^3$

7) $15x^4y^9$

8) $-30p^6q^8$

9) $48s^9t^9$

10) $-32x^{11}y^5$

11) $27xy^{10}z^3$

12) $24x^{13}y^5$

13) $-28p^5q^{13}$

14) $-45s^5t^7$

15) $-40p^7q^{11}$

16) $-35p^3q^9r^4$

17) $36a^{11}b^8c^4$

18) $-35u^{17}v^{16}$

19) $-20u^5v^{17}z^3$

20) $-18x^4y^4z^{12}$

21) $-42x^6y^5z^6$

22) $28a^{11}b^{13}c^{21}$

Multiplying and Dividing Monomials

1) $6x^7$

2) $12x^9$

3) $-14x^{14}$

4) $-35x^{13}y^{15}$

5) $24x^7y^{11}$

6) $56y^6x^5$

7) $8x^4y^4$

8) $18x^{15}y^{12}$

9) $30x^{12}y^7$

10) $-56x^{12}y^4$

11) $54x^{13}y^6$

12) $48x^{14}y^9$

13) $-35x^{15}y^{17}$

14) $30x^5y^7$

15) $36x^{12}y^{21}$

16) $-20x^{21}y^{13}$

17) $6x^4y$

18) $3x^2y^5$

19) $4x^3y^5$

20) $-6x^4y^4$

Multiplying a Polynomial and a Monomial

1) $x^2 - 5x$

2) $2x + 6$

3) $x^2 - 7x$

4) $x^2 + 9x$

5) $2x^2 - 4x$

6) $20x + 15$

7) $12x^2 - 16x$

8) $5x^2 + 2xy$

9) $3x^2 - 6xy$

10) $18x^2 - 24xy$

11) $6x^2 - 16x$

12) $24x^2 - 36xy$

13) $12x^2 - 6xy$

14) $4x^2 - 12xy$

15) $5x^3 + 5xy^2$

16) $6x^3 - 3xy^2$

17) $54x^2 + 18y^2$

18) $-12x^3y + 8xy$

19) $-18x^2 + 15xy - 9$

20) $6x^2 - 24xy - 18$

Multiplying Binomials

1) $x^2 + x - 12$

2) $x^2 + 8x + 15$

3) $x^2 - 13x + 42$

4) $x^2 - 13x + 36$

5) $x^2 - 12x + 35$

6) $x^2 + 8x + 12$

7) $x^2 - 6x - 27$

8) $x^2 - 13x + 40$

9) $x^2 + 10x + 21$

10) $x^2 - 5x - 36$

11) $x^2 + 12x + 36$

12) $x^2 + 14x + 49$

13) $x^2 - x - 56$

14) $x^2 + 18x + 81$

15) $x^2 - 16x + 64$

16) $x^2 - 4x - 45$

17) $2x^2 + 3x - 20$

18) $2x^2 + 12x + 18$

19) $2x^2 + 14x + 20$

20) $4x^2 - 2x - 6$

Factoring Trinomials

1) $(x + 4)(x + 1)$

2) $(x + 3)(x + 2)$

3) $(x - 1)(x - 3)$

4) $(x - 5)(x - 5)$

5) $(x - 8)(x - 5)$

6) $(x + 6)(x + 2)$

7) $(x - 9)(x + 3)$

8) $(x - 8)(x - 6)$

9) $(x + 8)(x + 7)$

10) $(x - 9)(x + 4)$

11) $(x + 6)(x + 6)$

12) $(x + 7)(x + 9)$

13) $(x - 8)(x + 9)$

14) $(x + 9)(x + 9)$

15) $(x - 8)(x - 8)$

16) $(x - 9)(x - 9)$

17) $2(x + 1)(x + 4)$

18) $2(x - 1)(x + 3)$

19) $(2x + 1)(x + 4)$

20) $(2x - 4)(2x + 6)$

Chapter 11: Geometry and Solid Figures

Math Topics that you'll learn in this Chapter:

- ✓ The Pythagorean Theorem
- ✓ Triangles
- ✓ Polygons
- ✓ Circles
- ✓ Trapezoids
- ✓ Cubes
- ✓ Rectangle Prisms
- ✓ Cylinder

105

The Pythagorean Theorem

✍ *Do the following lengths form a right triangle?*

1) _____

3
6
4

2) _____

9
10
6

3) _____

16
9
10

4) _____

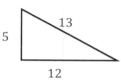

5
13
12

5) _____

9
12
4

6) _____

5
20
14

7) _____

15
25
20

8) _____

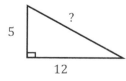

13
5
12

✍ *Find the missing side.*

9) _____

20
?
15

10) _____

16
20
?

11) _____

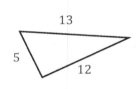

10
?
8

12) _____

?
16
30

13) _____

8
?
6

14) _____

3
?
4

15) _____

5
?
12

16) _____

?
15
20

Chapter 11: Geometry and Solid Figures

Triangles

Find the measure of the unknown angle in each triangle.

1) _____

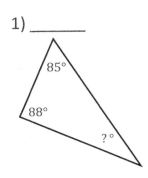

85°
88°
? °

2) _____

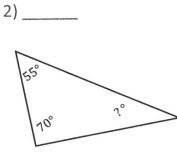

55°
70°
? °

3) _____

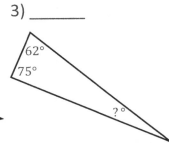

62°
75°
? °

4) _____

55°
70°   ? °

5) _____

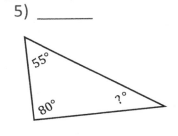

55°
80°   ? °

6) _____

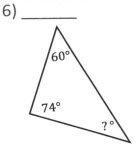

60°
74°
? °

7) _____

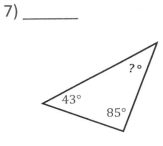

? °
43°
85°

8) _____

35°
74°   ? °

Find area of each triangle.

9) _____

11
6
9

10) _____

13
12
9

11) _____

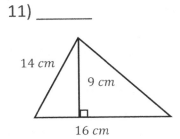

14 cm
9 cm
16 cm

12) _____

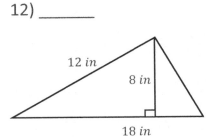

12 in
8 in
18 in

www.EffortlessMath.com

Polygons

✍ *Find the perimeter of each shape.*

1) (square) _____

6 cm

2) _____

12 m

8 m   8 m

12 m

3) _____

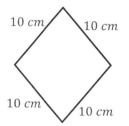

10 cm   10 cm

10 cm   10 cm

4) (square) _____

8 m

5) (regular hexagon) _____

16 m

6) _____

14 m

12 m   12 m

18 m

7) (parallelogram) _____

6 cm

8 cm

8) (regular hexagon) _____

20 ft

9) _____

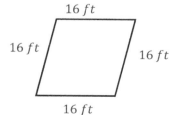

16 ft

16 ft   16 ft

16 ft

10) _____

22 in

18 in   18 in

22 in

11) _____

15 ft   15 ft

15 ft   15 ft

12) (regular hexagon) _____

30 in

Circles

✍️ *Find the Circumference of each circle.* (π = 3.14)

1) ____   2) ____   3) ____   4) ____   5) ____   6) ____

7) ____   8) ____   9) ____   10) ____   11) ____   12) ____

✍️ *Complete the table below.* (π = 3.14)

	Radius	Diameter	Circumference	Area
Circle 1	2 inches	4 inches	12.56 inches	12.56 square inches
Circle 2		8 meters		
Circle 3				113.04 square feet
Circle 4			50.24 miles	
Circle 5		9 kilometers		
Circle 6	7 centimeters			
Circle 7		18 feet		
Circle 8				78.5 square meters
Circle 9			69.08 inches	
Circle 10	10 feet			

Cubes

✍ *Find the volume of each cube.*

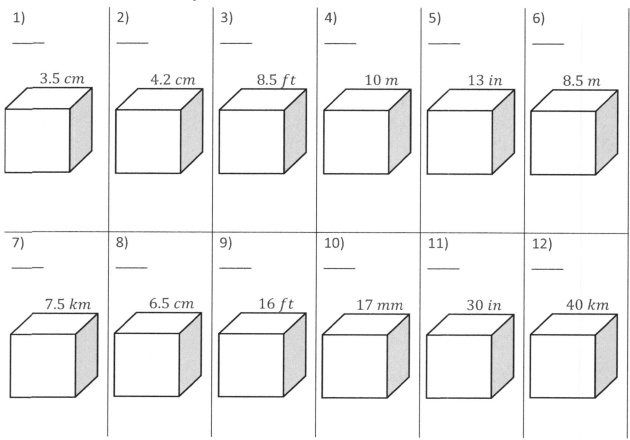

1) ___	2) ___	3) ___	4) ___	5) ___	6) ___
3.5 cm	4.2 cm	8.5 ft	10 m	13 in	8.5 m

7) ___	8) ___	9) ___	10) ___	11) ___	12) ___
7.5 km	6.5 cm	16 ft	17 mm	30 in	40 km

✍ *Find the surface area of each cube.*

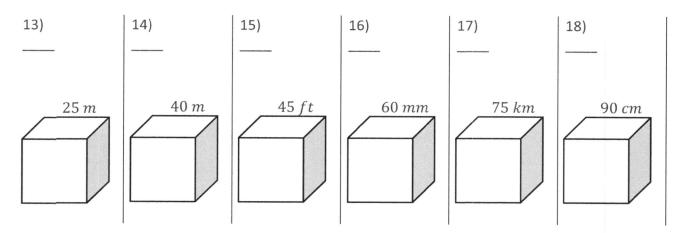

13) ___	14) ___	15) ___	16) ___	17) ___	18) ___
25 m	40 m	45 ft	60 mm	75 km	90 cm

Trapezoids

 Find the area of each trapezoid.

1) _____

12 cm

8 cm

14 cm

2) _____

16 m

12 m

20 m

3) _____

8 ft

6 ft

10 ft

4) _____

9 cm

6 cm

12 cm

5) _____

4 cm

6 cm

12 cm

6) _____

12 in

8 in

16 in

7) _____

20 cm

16 cm

24 cm

8) _____

18 in

14 in

22 in

 Solve.

9) A trapezoid has an area of $78\ cm^2$ and its height is $10\ cm$ and one base is $8\ cm$. What is the other base length? _____

10) If a trapezoid has an area of $160\ ft^2$ and the lengths of the bases are $12\ ft$ and $8\ ft$, find the height. _____

11) If a trapezoid has an area of $180\ m^2$ and its height is $8\ m$ and one base is $10\ m$, find the other base length. _____

12) The area of a trapezoid is $150\ ft^2$ and its height is $20\ ft$. If one base of the trapezoid is $12\ ft$, what is the other base length? _____

Rectangular Prisms

✍ *Find the volume of each Rectangular Prism.*

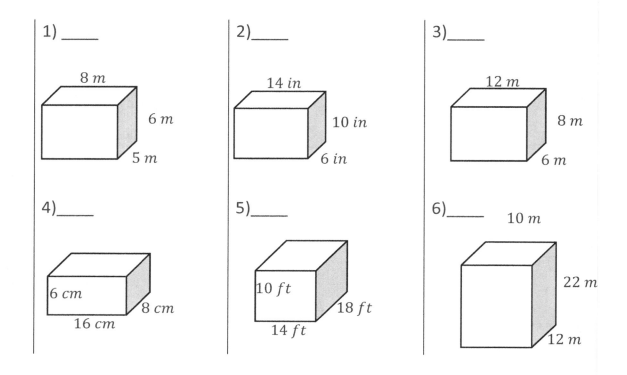

1) ____

8 m
6 m
5 m

2) ____

14 in
10 in
6 in

3) ____

12 m
8 m
6 m

4) ____

6 cm
8 cm
16 cm

5) ____

10 ft
18 ft
14 ft

6) ____

10 m
22 m
12 m

✍ *Find the surface area of each Rectangular Prism.*

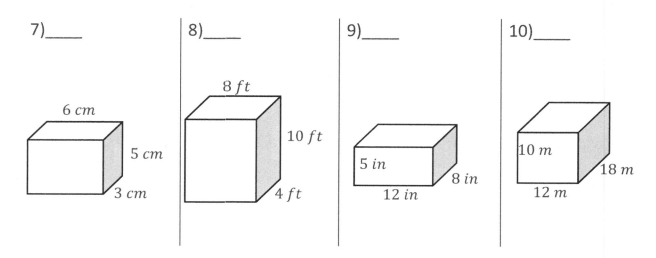

7) ____

6 cm
5 cm
3 cm

8) ____

8 ft
10 ft
4 ft

9) ____

5 in
8 in
12 in

10) ____

10 m
18 m
12 m

Cylinder

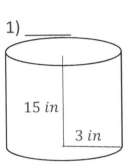 **Find the volume of each Cylinder.** ($\pi = 3.14$)

1) _____

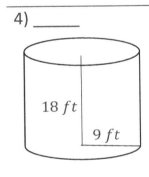

15 in

3 in

2) _____

9 cm

5 cm

3) _____

15 in

8 in

4) _____

18 ft

9 ft

5) _____

18 in

8 in

6) _____

22 in

12 in

 Find the surface area of each Cylinder. ($\pi = 3.14$)

7) _____

12 in

4 in

8) _____

9 cm

5 cm

9) _____

14 ft

6 ft

10) _____

15 m

5 m

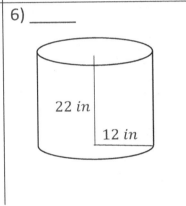

Answers – Chapter 11

The Pythagorean Theorem

1) *no*

2) *no*

3) *no*

4) *yes*

5) *no*

6) *no*

7) *yes*

8) *yes*

9) 25

10) 12

11) 6

12) 34

13) 10

14) 5

15) 13

16) 25

Triangles

1) 7°

2) 55°

3) 43°

4) 55°

5) 45°

6) 46°

7) 52°

8) 71°

9) 27

10) 54

11) 72 cm^2

12) 72 in^2

Polygons

1) 24 cm

2) 40 m

3) 40 cm

4) 32 m

5) 96 m

6) 56 m

7) 28 cm

8) 120 ft

9) 64 ft

10) 80 in

11) 60 ft

12) 180 in

Circles

1) 37.68 *in*

2) 62.8 *cm*

3) 119.32 *ft*

4) 75.36 *m*

5) 113.04 *cm*

6) 94.2 *miles*

7) 119.32 *in*

8) 138.16 *ft*

9) 157 *m*

10) 175.84 *m*

11) 219.8 *in*

12) 314 *ft*

	Radius	Diameter	Circumference	Area
Circle 1	2 inches	4 inches	12.56 inches	12.56 square inches
Circle 2	4 meters	8 meters	25.12 meters	50.24 square meters
Circle 3	6 feet	12 feet	37.68 feet	113.04 square feet
Circle 4	8 miles	16 miles	50.24 miles	200.96 square miles
Circle 5	4.5 kilometers	9 kilometers	28.26 kilometers	63.585 square kilometers
Circle 6	7 centimeters	14 centimeters	43.96 centimeters	153.86 square centimeters
Circle 7	9 feet	18 feet	56.52 feet	254.34 square feet
Circle 8	5 meters	10 meters	31.4 meters	78.5 square meters
Circle 9	11 inches	22 inches	69.08 inches	379.94 square inches
Circle 10	10 feet	20 feet	62.8 feet	314 square feet

Cubes

1) $42.875 \ cm^3$

2) $74.088 \ cm^3$

3) $614.125 \ ft^3$

4) $1,000 \ m^3$

5) $2,197 \ in^3$

6) $614.125 \ m^3$

7) $421.875 \ km^3$

8) $274.625 \ cm^3$

9) $4,096 \ ft^3$

10) $4,913 \ mm^3$

11) $27,000 \ in^3$

12) $64,000 \ km^3$

13) $3,750 \ m^2$

14) $9,600 \ m^2$

15) $12,150 \ ft^2$

16) $21,600 \ mm^2$

17) $33,750 \ km^2$

18) $48,600 \ cm^2$

Trapezoids

1) $104 \; cm^2$

2) $216 \; m^2$

3) $54 \; ft^2$

4) $63 \; cm^2$

5) $48 \; cm^2$

6) $112 \; in^2$

7) $352 \; cm^2$

8) $280 \; in^2$

9) $7.6 \; cm$

10) $16 \; ft$

11) $35 \; m$

12) $3 \; ft$

Rectangular Prisms

1) $240 \; m^3$

2) $840 \; in^3$

3) $576 \; m^3$

4) $768 \; cm^3$

5) $2,520 \; ft^3$

6) $2,640 \; m^3$

7) $126 \; cm^2$

8) $304 \; ft^2$

9) $392 \; in^2$

10) $1,032 \; m^2$

Cylinder

1) $423.9 \; in^3$

2) $706.5 \; cm^3$

3) $3,014.4 \; in^3$

4) $4,578.12 \; ft^3$

5) $3,617.28 \; in^3$

6) $9,947.52 \; in^3$

7) $401.92 \; in^2$

8) $439.6 \; cm^2$

9) $753.6 \; ft^2$

10) $628 \; m^2$

Chapter 12: Statistics

Math Topics that you'll learn in this Chapter:

- ✓ Mean, Median, Mode, and Range of the Given Data
- ✓ Pie Graph
- ✓ Probability Problems
- ✓ Permutations and Combinations

117

Mean, Median, Mode, and Range of the Given Data

✍ *Find the values of the Given Data.*

1) 5, 12, 2, 2, 6

Mode: _____   Range: _____

Mean: _____   Median: _____

2) 5, 9, 3, 6, 4, 3

Mode: _____   Range: _____

Mean: _____   Median: _____

3) 12, 5, 8, 7, 8

Mode: _____   Range: _____

Mean: _____   Median: _____

4) 9, 7, 12, 7, 3, 4

Mode: _____   Range: _____

Mean: _____   Median: _____

5) 9, 7, 10, 5, 7, 4, 14

Mode: _____   Range: _____

Mean: _____   Median: _____

6) 8, 1, 6, 6, 9, 2, 17

Mode: _____   Range: _____

Mean: _____   Median: _____

7) 14, 5, 2, 7, 10, 7, 8, 13

Mode: _____   Range: _____

Mean: _____   Median: _____

8) 12, 14, 6, 4, 10, 8, 2

Mode: _____   Range: _____

Mean: _____   Median: _____

9) 17, 13, 16, 12, 14, 24

Mode: _____   Range: _____

Mean: _____   Median: _____

10) 18, 15, 10, 8, 4, 7, 8, 18

Mode: _____   Range: _____

Mean: _____   Median: _____

Pie Graph

The circle graph below shows all Wilson's expenses for last month. Wilson spent $300 *on his bills last month.*

Answer following questions based on the Pie graph.

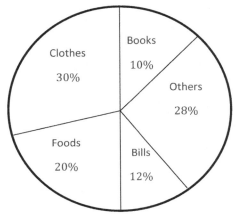

Wilson's last month expenses

1) How much was Wilson's total expenses last month? _____

2) How much did Wilson spend on his clothes last month? _____

3) How much did Wilson spend for foods last month? _____

4) How much did Wilson spend on his books last month? _____

5) What fraction is Wilson's expenses for his bills and clothes out of his total

   expenses last month? _____

Probability Problems

1) If there are 15 red balls and 30 blue balls in a basket, what is the probability that Oliver will pick out a red ball from the basket? _____

Gender	Under 45	45 or older	Total
Male	12	6	18
Female	5	7	12
Total	17	13	30

2) The table above shows the distribution of age and gender for 30 employees in a company. If one employee is selected at random, what is the probability that the employee selected be either a female under age 45 or a male age 45 or older? _____

3) A number is chosen at random from 1 to 18. Find the probability of not selecting a composite number. (A composite number is a number that is divisible by itself, 1 and at least one other whole number) _____

4) There are 6 blue marbles, 8 red marbles, and 5 yellow marbles in a box. If Ava randomly selects a marble from the box, what is the probability of selecting a red or yellow marble? _____

5) A bag contains 20 balls: three green, six black, eight blue, a brown, a red and one white. If 19 balls are removed from the bag at random, what is the probability that a brown ball has been removed? _____

6) There are only red and blue marbles in a box. The probability of choosing a red marble in the box at random is one third. If there are 160 blue marbles, how many marbles are in the box? _____

Chapter 12: Statistics

Permutations and Combinations

✍ *Calculate the value of each.*

1) $5! = \underline{\hspace{1cm}}$

2) $6! = \underline{\hspace{1cm}}$

3) $8! = \underline{\hspace{1cm}}$

4) $5! + 6! = \underline{\hspace{1cm}}$

5) $8! + 3! = \underline{\hspace{1cm}}$

6) $6! + 7! = \underline{\hspace{1cm}}$

7) $8! + 4! = \underline{\hspace{1cm}}$

8) $9! - 3! = \underline{\hspace{1cm}}$

✍ *Solve each word problems.*

9) Sophia is baking cookies. She uses milk, flour and eggs. How many different orders of ingredients can she try? $\underline{\hspace{1cm}}$

10) William is planning for his vacation. He wants to go to restaurant, watch a movie, go to the beach, and play basketball. How many different ways of ordering are there for him? $\underline{\hspace{1cm}}$

11) How many 7 −digit numbers can be named using the digits $1, 2, 3, 4, 5, 6$ and 7 without repetition? $\underline{\hspace{1cm}}$

12) In how many ways can 9 boys be arranged in a straight line? $\underline{\hspace{1cm}}$

13) In how many ways can 8 athletes be arranged in a straight line? $\underline{\hspace{1cm}}$

14) A professor is going to arrange her 6 students in a straight line. In how many ways can she do this? $\underline{\hspace{1cm}}$

15) How many code symbols can be formed with the letters for the word BLUE? $\underline{\hspace{1cm}}$

16) In how many ways a team of 8 basketball players can choose a captain and co-captain? $\underline{\hspace{1cm}}$

Answers – Chapter 12

Mean, Median, Mode, and Range of the Given Data

1) Mode: 2   Range: 10   Mean: 5.4   Median: 5

2) Mode: 3   Range: 6   Mean: 5   Median: 4.5

3) Mode: 8   Range: 7   Mean: 8   Median: 8

4) Mode: 7   Range: 9   Mean: 7   Median: 7

5) Mode: 7   Range: 10   Mean: 8   Median: 7

6) Mode: 6   Range: 16   Mean: 7   Median: 6

7) Mode: 7   Range: 12   Mean: 8.25   Median: 7.5

8) Mode: *no mode*   Range: 12   Mean: 8   Median: 8

9) Mode: *no mode*   Range: 12   Mean: 16   Median: 15

10) Mode: 8,18   Range: 14   Mean: 11   Median: 9

Pie Graph

1) $2,500

2) $750

3) $500

4) $250

5) $\frac{21}{50}$

Probability Problems

1) $\frac{1}{3}$

2) $\frac{11}{30}$

3) $\frac{7}{18}$

4) $\frac{13}{19}$

5) $\frac{19}{20}$

6) 240

Permutations and Combinations

1) 120

2) 720

3) 40,320

4) 840

5) 40,326

6) 5,760

7) 40,344

8) 362,874

9) 6

10) 24

11) 5,040

12) 362,880

13) 40,320

14) 720

15) 24

16) 56

Chapter 13:
Functions Operations

Math Topics that you'll learn in this Chapter:

- ✓ Function Notation and Evaluation
- ✓ Adding and Subtracting Functions
- ✓ Multiplying and Dividing Functions
- ✓ Composition of Functions

Function Notation and Evaluation

✎ *Evaluate each function.*

1) $f(x) = x - 3$, find $f(-2)$

_____

2) $g(x) = x + 5$, find $g(6)$

_____

3) $h(x) = x + 8$, find $h(2)$

_____

4) $f(x) = -x - 7$, find $f(5)$

_____

5) $f(x) = 2x - 7$, find $f(-1)$

_____

6) $w(x) = -2 - 4x$, find $w(5)$

_____

7) $g(n) = 6n - 3$, find $g(-2)$

_____

8) $h(x) = -8x + 12$, find $h(3)$

_____

9) $k(n) = 14 - 3n$, find $k(3)$

_____

10) $g(x) = 4x - 4$, find $g(-2)$

_____

11) $k(n) = 8n - 7$, find $k(4)$

_____

12) $w(n) = -2n + 14$, find $w(5)$

_____

13) $h(x) = 5x - 18$, find $h(8)$

_____

14) $g(n) = 2n^2 + 2$, find $g(5)$

_____

15) $f(x) = 3x^2 - 13$, find $f(2)$

_____

16) $g(n) = 5n^2 + 7$, find $g(-3)$

_____

17) $h(n) = 5n^2 - 10$, find $h(4)$

_____

18) $g(x) = -3x^2 - 6x$, find $g(2)$

_____

19) $k(n) = 4n^3 + n$, find $k(-5)$

_____

20) $f(x) = -3x + 10$, find $f(3x)$

_____

21) $k(a) = 4a + 9$, find $k(a - 1)$

_____

22) $h(x) = 8x + 4$, find $h(5x)$

_____

Adding and Subtracting Functions

✐ *Perform the indicated operation.*

1) $f(x) = x + 4$

$g(x) = 2x + 5$

Find $(f - g)(2)$

_____

2) $g(x) = x - 2$

$f(x) = -x - 6$

Find $(g - f)(-2)$

_____

3) $h(t) = 4t + 4$

$g(t) = 3t + 2$

Find $(h + g)(-1)$

_____

4) $g(a) = 5a - 7$

$f(a) = a^2 + 3$

Find $(g + f)(2)$

_____

5) $g(x) = 4x - 5$

$f(x) = 6x^2 + 5$

Find $(g - f)(-2)$

_____

6) $h(x) = x^2 + 3$

$g(x) = -4x + 1$

Find $(h + g)(4)$

_____

7) $f(x) = -3x - 9$

$g(x) = x^2 + 5$

Find $(f - g)(6)$

_____

8) $h(n) = -4n^2 + 9$

$g(n) = 5n + 6$

Find $(h - g)(5)$

_____

9) $g(x) = 4x^2 - 3x - 1$

$f(x) = 6x + 10$

Find $(g - f)(a)$

_____

10) $g(t) = -6t - 7$

$f(t) = -t^2 + 3t + 15$

Find $(g + f)(t)$

_____

Multiplying and Dividing Functions

✍ *Perform the indicated operation.*

1) $g(x) = x + 6$

   $f(x) = x + 4$

   Find $(g.f)(2)$

   _____

2) $f(x) = 3x$

   $h(x) = -x + 5$

   Find $(f.h)(-2)$

   _____

3) $g(a) = a + 5$

   $h(a) = 2a - 4$

   Find $(g.h)(4)$

   _____

4) $f(x) = 3x + 2$

   $h(x) = 2x - 3$

   Find $(\frac{f}{h})(2)$

   _____

5) $f(x) = a^2 - 2$

   $g(x) = -4 + 3a$

   Find $(\frac{f}{g})(2)$

   _____

6) $g(a) = 4a + 6$

   $f(a) = 2a - 8$

   Find $(\frac{g}{f})(3)$

   _____

7) $g(t) = t^2 + 6$

   $h(t) = 2t - 3$

   Find $(g.h)(-3)$

   _____

8) $g(x) = x^2 + 3x + 4$

   $h(x) = 2x + 6$

   Find $(g.h)(2)$

   _____

9) $g(a) = 2a^2 - 5a + 1$

   $f(a) = 2a^3 - 6$

   Find $(\frac{g}{f})(4)$

   _____

10) $g(x) = -3x^2 + 4 - 2x$

    $f(x) = x^2 - 5$

    Find $(g.f)(3)$

    _____

Composition of Functions

✎ **Using $f(x) = x + 6$ and $g(x) = 3x$, find:**

1) $f(g(1)) = $ ____

2) $f(g(-1)) = $ ____

3) $g(f(-3)) = $ ____

4) $g(f(4)) = $ ____

5) $f(g(2)) = $ ____

6) $g(f(3)) = $ ____

✎ **Using $f(x) = 2x + 5$ and $g(x) = x - 2$, find:**

7) $g(f(2)) = $ ____

8) $g(f(-2)) = $ ____

9) $f(g(5)) = $ ____

10) $f(f(4)) = $ ____

11) $g(f(3)) = $ ____

12) $g(f(-3)) = $ ____

✎ **Using $f(x) = 4x - 2$ and $g(x) = x - 5$, find:**

13) $g(f(-2)) = $ ____

14) $f(f(4)) = $ ____

15) $f(g(5)) = $ ____

16) $f(f(3)) = $ ____

17) $g(f(-3)) = $ ____

18) $g(g(6)) = $ ____

✎ **Using $f(x) = 6x + 2$ and $g(x) = 2x - 3$, find:**

19) $f(g(-3)) = $ ____

20) $g(f(5)) = $ ____

21) $f(g(4)) = $ ____

22) $f(f(3)) = $ ____

Answers – Chapter 13

Function Notation and Evaluation

1) -5

2) 11

3) 10

4) -12

5) -9

6) -22

7) -15

8) -12

9) 5

10) -12

11) 25

12) 4

13) 22

14) 52

15) -1

16) 52

17) 70

18) -24

19) -505

20) $-9x + 10$

21) $4a + 5$

22) $40x + 4$

Adding and Subtracting Functions

1) -3

2) 0

3) -1

4) 10

5) -42

6) 4

7) -68

8) -122

9) $4a^2 - 9a - 11$

10) $-t^2 - 3t + 8$

Multiplying and Dividing Functions

1) 48

2) -42

3) 36

4) 8

5) 1

6) -9

7) -135

8) 140

9) $\frac{13}{122}$

10) -116

Composition of Functions

1) $f(g(1)) = 9$

2) $f(g(-1)) = 3$

3) $g(f(-3)) = 9$

4) $g(f(4)) = 30$

5) $f(g(2)) = 12$

6) $g(f(3)) = 27$

7) $g(f(2)) = 7$

8) $g(f(-2)) = -1$

9) $f(g(5)) = 11$

10) $f(f(4)) = 31$

11) $g(f(3)) = 9$

12) $g(f(-3)) = -3$

13) $g(f(-2)) = -15$

14) $f(f(4)) = 54$

15) $f(g(5)) = -2$

16) $f(f(3)) = 38$

17) $g(f(-3)) = -19$

18) $g(g(6)) = -4$

19) $f(g(-3)) = -52$

20) $g(f(5)) = 61$

21) $f(g(4)) = 32$

22) $f(f(3)) = 122$

Time to Test

Time to refine your skill with a practice examination

Take practice CLEP College Mathematics Tests to simulate the test day experience. After you've finished, score your tests using the answer keys.

Before You Start

- You'll need a pencil, a calculator and a timer to take the test.

- For each question, there are four possible answers. Choose which one is best.

- It's okay to guess. There is no penalty for wrong answers.

- Use the answer sheet provided to record your answers.

- After you've finished the test, review the answer key to see where you went wrong.

Good Luck!

CLEP College Mathematics Practice Test 1

2022

Total number of questions: 60

Total time: 90 Minutes

Calculator is permitted for CLEP College

Mathematics Test.

133

CLEP College Mathematics Practice Test Answer Sheet

Remove (or photocopy) this answer sheet and use it to complete the practice test.

CLEP College Mathematics Practice Test 1			
1 Ⓐ Ⓑ Ⓒ Ⓓ	16 Ⓐ Ⓑ Ⓒ Ⓓ	31 Ⓐ Ⓑ Ⓒ Ⓓ	46 Ⓐ Ⓑ Ⓒ Ⓓ
2 Ⓐ Ⓑ Ⓒ Ⓓ	17 Ⓐ Ⓑ Ⓒ Ⓓ	32 Ⓐ Ⓑ Ⓒ Ⓓ	47 Ⓐ Ⓑ Ⓒ Ⓓ
3 Ⓐ Ⓑ Ⓒ Ⓓ	18 Ⓐ Ⓑ Ⓒ Ⓓ	33 Ⓐ Ⓑ Ⓒ Ⓓ	48 Ⓐ Ⓑ Ⓒ Ⓓ
4 Ⓐ Ⓑ Ⓒ Ⓓ	19 Ⓐ Ⓑ Ⓒ Ⓓ	34 Ⓐ Ⓑ Ⓒ Ⓓ	39 Ⓐ Ⓑ Ⓒ Ⓓ
5 Ⓐ Ⓑ Ⓒ Ⓓ	20 Ⓐ Ⓑ Ⓒ Ⓓ	35 Ⓐ Ⓑ Ⓒ Ⓓ	50 Ⓐ Ⓑ Ⓒ Ⓓ
6 Ⓐ Ⓑ Ⓒ Ⓓ	21 Ⓐ Ⓑ Ⓒ Ⓓ	36 Ⓐ Ⓑ Ⓒ Ⓓ	51 Ⓐ Ⓑ Ⓒ Ⓓ
7 Ⓐ Ⓑ Ⓒ Ⓓ	22 Ⓐ Ⓑ Ⓒ Ⓓ	37 Ⓐ Ⓑ Ⓒ Ⓓ	52 Ⓐ Ⓑ Ⓒ Ⓓ
8 Ⓐ Ⓑ Ⓒ Ⓓ	23 Ⓐ Ⓑ Ⓒ Ⓓ	38 Ⓐ Ⓑ Ⓒ Ⓓ	53 Ⓐ Ⓑ Ⓒ Ⓓ
9 Ⓐ Ⓑ Ⓒ Ⓓ	24 Ⓐ Ⓑ Ⓒ Ⓓ	39 Ⓐ Ⓑ Ⓒ Ⓓ	54 Ⓐ Ⓑ Ⓒ Ⓓ
10 Ⓐ Ⓑ Ⓒ Ⓓ	25 Ⓐ Ⓑ Ⓒ Ⓓ	40 Ⓐ Ⓑ Ⓒ Ⓓ	55 Ⓐ Ⓑ Ⓒ Ⓓ
11 Ⓐ Ⓑ Ⓒ Ⓓ	26 Ⓐ Ⓑ Ⓒ Ⓓ	41 Ⓐ Ⓑ Ⓒ Ⓓ	56 Ⓐ Ⓑ Ⓒ Ⓓ
12 Ⓐ Ⓑ Ⓒ Ⓓ	27 Ⓐ Ⓑ Ⓒ Ⓓ	42 Ⓐ Ⓑ Ⓒ Ⓓ	57 Ⓐ Ⓑ Ⓒ Ⓓ
13 Ⓐ Ⓑ Ⓒ Ⓓ	28 Ⓐ Ⓑ Ⓒ Ⓓ	43 Ⓐ Ⓑ Ⓒ Ⓓ	58 Ⓐ Ⓑ Ⓒ Ⓓ
14 Ⓐ Ⓑ Ⓒ Ⓓ	29 Ⓐ Ⓑ Ⓒ Ⓓ	44 Ⓐ Ⓑ Ⓒ Ⓓ	59 Ⓐ Ⓑ Ⓒ Ⓓ
15 Ⓐ Ⓑ Ⓒ Ⓓ	30 Ⓐ Ⓑ Ⓒ Ⓓ	45 Ⓐ Ⓑ Ⓒ Ⓓ	60 Ⓐ Ⓑ Ⓒ Ⓓ

1) If $f(x) = 3x^3 + 5x^2 + 2x$ and $g(x) = -2$, what is the value of $f(g(x))$?

A. 36

B. 32

C. 24

D. -8

2) Jennifer drank 2 glasses of water. There was $\frac{2}{7}$ ml of water in the first glass and $\frac{3}{8}$ ml in the second glass. How much water did Jennifer drink?

A. $\frac{3}{4}$ ml

B. $\frac{11}{28}$ ml

C. $\frac{25}{56}$ ml

D. $\frac{37}{56}$ ml

3) If $x = \frac{1}{3}$ and $y = \frac{9}{21}$, then which is equal to $\frac{1}{x} \div \frac{y}{3}$?

A. $\frac{1}{7}$

B. $\frac{1}{21}$

C. $\frac{1}{3}$

D. 21

4) A piece of paper that is $2\frac{3}{5}$ feet long is cut into 2 pieces of different lengths. The shorter piece has a length of x feet. Which inequality expresses all possible values of x?

A. $x > 2$

B. $x < 1\frac{3}{10}$

C. $x < 2\frac{1}{10}$

D. $x < 2\frac{3}{5}$

5) Which of the following answers represents the compound inequality $-4 \leq 4x - 8 < 16$?

A. $-2 \leq x \leq 8$

B. $-2 < x \leq 8$

C. $1 < x \leq 6$

D. $1 \leq x < 6$

6) A shoes originally priced at $45.00 was on sale for 15% off. Nick received a 20% employee discount applied to the sale price. How much did Nick pay for the shoes?
A. $30.60

B. $34.50

C. $37.30

D. $42.25

7) Mr. Carlos family are choosing a menu for their reception. They have 3 choices of appetizers, 7 choices of entrees, 4 choices of cake. How many different menu combinations are possible for them to choose?
A. 12

B. 32

C. 84

D. 120

8) The volume of a cube is less than $64 \ m^3$. Which of the following can be the cube's side?
A. $2 \ m$

B. $4 \ m$

C. $8 \ m$

D. $11 \ m$

9) How many hours are there in 1,800 minutes?
A. 20 hours

B. 25 hours

C. 30 hours

D. 33 hours

10) The following graph shows the mark of seven students in mathematics. What is the mean (average) of the marks?
A. 13.5

B. 14

C. 14.5

D. 15

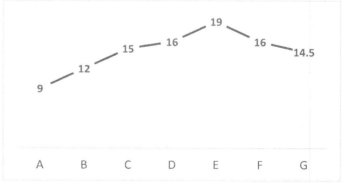

11) Jack scored a mean of 80 per test in his first 4 tests. In his 5th test, he scored 90. What was Jack's mean score for the 5 tests?

A. 70

B. 75

C. 80

D. 82

12) The ratio of boys and girls in a class is 4: 7. If there are 66 students in the class, how many more boys should be enrolled to make the ratio 1: 1?

A. 8

B. 10

C. 12

D. 18

13) Jack earns $616 for his first 44 hours of work in a week and is then paid 1.5 times his regular hourly rate for any additional hours. This week, Jack needs $826 to pay his rent, bills and other expenses. How many hours must he work to make enough money in this week?

A. 40

B. 43

C. 48

D. 54

14) The least of 8 consecutive integers is m, and the greatest is n. What is the value of $\frac{m+n}{3}$ in terms of m?

A. $m + 1$

B. $2m + 8$

C. $\frac{2m+7}{3}$

D. $\frac{2m}{7}$

15) Anna opened an account with a deposit of $3,000. This account earns 5% simple interest annually. How many years will it take her to earn $600 on her $3,000 deposit?

A. 2

B. 4

C. 5

D. 8

16) Simplify the expression. $(5x^3 - 8x^2 + 2x^4) - (4x^2 - 2x^4 + 2x^3)$
   A. $4x^4 + 3x^3 - 12x^2$

   B. $5x^4 + x^3 - 9x^2$

   C. $5x^4 + 2x^3 - 8x^2$

   D. $8x^4 + 7x^3 - 8x^2$

17) If $360\ kg$ of vegetables is packed in 90 boxes, how much vegetables will each box contain?
   A. $2.5\ kg$

   B. $3\ kg$

   C. $4\ kg$

   D. $6.5\ kg$

18) A certain insect has a mass of 85 milligrams. What is the insect's mass in grams?
   A. 85

   B. 0.85

   C. 0.08

   D. 0.085

19) Tomas is 6 feet 8.5 inches tall, and Alex is 5 feet 3 inches tall. What is the difference in height, in inches, between Alex and Tomas?
   A. 2.5

   B. 7.5

   C. 12.5

   D. 17.5

20) In an academy, course grades range from 0 to 100. Anna took 5 courses and her mean course grade was 80. William took 8 courses. If both students have the same sum of course grades, what was William's mean?
   A. 50

   B. 65

   C. 70

   D. 85

21) The price of a Chocolate was raised from $5.40 to $5.67. What was the percent increase in the price?

A. 4%

B. 5%

C. 6%

D. 8%

22) Scarlett played 5 games and had a mean score of 159. Mary played 3 games and had score of 95. What was the mean of the scores for all 8 games?

A. 118

B. 122

C. 131

D. 135

23) What is the area of an isosceles right triangle that has one leg that measures $6\ cm$?

A. $6\ cm^2$

B. $12\ cm^2$

C. $18\ cm^2$

D. $36\ cm^2$

24) In the xy-plane, the point $(4,3)$ and $(3,2)$ are on line A. Which of the following points could also be on line A?

A. $(-1,2)$

B. $(5,7)$

C. $(3,4)$

D. $(-1,-2)$

25) How many integers are between $\frac{7}{2}$ and $\frac{30}{4}$?

A. 3

B. 4

C. 6

D. 10

26) The shaded sector of the circle shown below has an area of 12π square feet. What is the circumference of the circle?

A. 24π feet

B. 81π feet

C. 124π feet

D. 180π feet

27) In the figure below, what is the value of x?

A. 8

B. 11

C. 15

D. 16

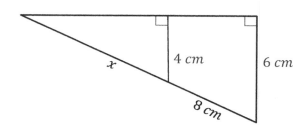

28) Which of the following is a factor of 45?

A. 7

B. 9

C. 11

D. 13

29) On the number line below, point M is located on line segment ON so that $OM = \frac{1}{3}MN$. What is the position of point M?

A. 1.5

B. -1.5

C. -3.5

D. -4.2

30) Which of the following equations has a graph that is a straight line?

A. $y = 3x^2 + 9$

B. $x^2 + y^2 = 1$

C. $4x - 2y = 2x$

D. $7x + 2xy = 6$

31) $8\frac{4}{7} \times 2\frac{2}{3} =$

  A. $20\frac{6}{7}$

  B. $22\frac{6}{7}$

  C. $24\frac{6}{7}$

  D. $26\frac{6}{7}$

32) Sarah walks $3\ km$ in one hour. How long does it take Sarah to walk $12\ km$ at this rate?

  A. 2 hours

  B. 3 hours

  C. 4 hours

  D. 5 hours

33) Yesterday Kylie writes 10% of her homework. Today she writes another 18% of the entire homework. What fraction of the homework is left for her to write?

  A. $\frac{4}{25}$

  B. $\frac{7}{25}$

  C. $\frac{10}{25}$

  D. $\frac{18}{25}$

34) If the function $g(x)$ has three distinct zeros, which of the following could represent the graph of $g(x)$?

  A.

  B.

  C.

  D.

35) If the area of trapezoid is 126, what is the perimeter of the trapezoid? (Figure not drawn to scale.)

A. 12 *cm*

B. 32 *cm*

C. 46 *cm*

D. 55 *cm*

36) A box contains 6 green sticks, 4 blue sticks, and 2 yellow sticks. Emma picks one without looking. What is the probability that the stick will be green?

A. $\frac{1}{2}$

B. $\frac{1}{3}$

C. $\frac{1}{4}$

D. $\frac{2}{5}$

37) Removing which of the following numbers will change the average of the numbers to 6?

$$1, 4, 5, 8, 11, 12$$

A. 1

B. 4

C. 5

D. 11

38) The capacity of a red box is 20% bigger than the capacity of a blue box. If the red box can hold 60 equal sized books, how many of the same books can the blue box hold?

A. 15

B. 25

C. 40

D. 50

39) If $(x - 2)^2 + 1 > 3x - 1$, then x can equal which of the following?

A. 1

B. 6

C. 8

D. 3

40) If one angle of a right triangle measures $60°$, what is the sine of the other acute angle?

A. $\dfrac{1}{2}$

B. $\dfrac{\sqrt{2}}{2}$

C. $\dfrac{\sqrt{3}}{2}$

D. 1

41) If $0.00104 = \dfrac{104}{x}$, what is the value of x?

A. $1,000$

B. $10,000$

C. $100,000$

D. $1,000,000$

42) $(x^6)^{\frac{7}{8}}$ is equal to …

A. $x^{\frac{19}{4}}$

B. $x^{\frac{21}{4}}$

C. $x^{\frac{23}{4}}$

D. $x^{\frac{25}{4}}$

43) Solve the following equation for y?
$$\frac{x}{5} = \frac{y-x}{4}$$

A. $\dfrac{1}{5}x$

B. $\dfrac{9}{5}x$

C. $5x$

D. $-x$

44) The ratio of two sides of a parallelogram is $2 : 3$. If its perimeter is $40\ cm$, find the length of its sides.

A. $8\ cm, 12\ cm$

B. $10\ cm, 14\ cm$

C. $12\ cm, 16\ cm$

D. $14\ cm, 18\ cm$

45) If $\frac{2y}{x} - \frac{y}{3x} = \frac{(\dots)}{3x}$ and $x \neq 0$, what expression is represented by $(\dots)$?

A. $2y + 4$

B. $3y - 6$

C. $5y$

D. $6y$

46) Ella (E) is 4 years older than her friend Ava (A) who is 3 years younger than her sister Sofia (S). If E, A and S denote their ages, which one of the following represents the given information?

A. $\begin{cases} E = A + 4 \\ S = A - 3 \end{cases}$

B. $\begin{cases} E = A + 4 \\ A = S + 3 \end{cases}$

C. $\begin{cases} A = E + 4 \\ S = A - 3 \end{cases}$

D. $\begin{cases} E = A + 4 \\ A = S - 3 \end{cases}$

47) The sum of two consecutive integer is -13. If 2 is added to the smaller integer and 3 is subtract from the larger integer, what is the product of the two resulting integers?

A. 5

B. 18

C. 28

D. 45

48) What is the sum of all values of n that satisfies $2n^2 + 16n + 24 = 0$?

A. 8

B. 4

C. -4

D. -8

49) The length of a rectangle is $\frac{4}{5}$ times its width. If the width is 30, what is the perimeter of this rectangle?

A. 26

B. 58

C. 72

D. 108

50) The arrow starts on space O and moves clockwise around the circle. It moves through one space each minute. What space will the arrow point to in 140 minutes?

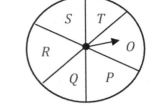

  A. O

  B. P

  C. Q

  D. R

51) If $x = 25$, then which of the following equations are correct?

  A. $x + 10 = 40$

  B. $4x = 100$

  C. $3x = 70$

  D. $\frac{x}{2} = 12$

52) Which graph best represents the following chart?

x	-4	4	-2
y	-2	2	1

A.

B.

D.

E.

53) Which of the following is equivalent to $\dfrac{x+(5x)^2+(3x)^3}{x}$?

   A. $16x^2 + 25x + 1$

   B. $27x^2 + 25x + 1$

   C. $16x^2 + 25x$

   D. $16x^3 - 16x^2 + 1$

54) In a coordinate plane, triangle ABC has coordinates: $(-1,6)$, $(-2,5)$, and $(5,8)$. If triangle ABC is reflected over the y-axis, what are the coordinates of the new image?

   A. $(-1,-6), (-2,-5), (-5,-8)$

   B. $(-1,-6), (-2,-5), (5,-8)$

   C. $(1,6), (2,5), (5,8)$

   D. $(1,6), (2,5), (-5,8)$

55) What is the difference in area between a $9\ cm$ by $4\ cm$ rectangle and a circle with diameter of $10\ cm$? ($\pi = 3$)

   A. 4

   B. 6

   C. 39

   D. 49

56) What is the solution of the following inequality?
$$|x - 2| \geq 3$$

   A. $x \geq 5 \cup x \leq -1$

   B. $-1 \leq x \leq 5$

   C. $x \geq 5$

   D. $x \leq -1$

57) If $x \neq 0$ and $x = x^{-6}$, what is the value of x?

   A. 1

   B. 2

   C. -2

   D. 3

58) In the following figure, ABCD is a rectangle. If $a = \sqrt{3}$, and $b = 2a$, find the area of the shaded region. (the shaded region is a trapezoid)

   A. 2

   B. 4

   C. $\sqrt{3}$

   D. $4\sqrt{3}$

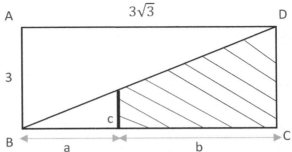

59) In the figure below, line A is parallel to line B. what is the value of x?

   A. 28

   B. 46

   C. 50

   D. 65

60) If Anna multiplies her age by 5 and then adds 3, she will get a number equal to her mother's age. If x is her mother's age, what is Anna's age in terms of x?

   A. $\frac{x-3}{5}$

   B. $\frac{x-5}{3}$

   C. $3x + 5$

   D. $5x - 3$

End of CLEP College Mathematics Practice Test 1

CLEP College Mathematics Practice Test 2

2022

Total number of questions: 60

Total time: 90 Minutes

Calculator is permitted for CLEP College Mathematics Test.

149

CLEP College Mathematics Practice Test Answer Sheet

Remove (or photocopy) this answer sheet and use it to complete the practice test.

CLEP College Mathematics Practice Test 2			
1 Ⓐ Ⓑ Ⓒ Ⓓ	16 Ⓐ Ⓑ Ⓒ Ⓓ	31 Ⓐ Ⓑ Ⓒ Ⓓ	46 Ⓐ Ⓑ Ⓒ Ⓓ
2 Ⓐ Ⓑ Ⓒ Ⓓ	17 Ⓐ Ⓑ Ⓒ Ⓓ	32 Ⓐ Ⓑ Ⓒ Ⓓ	47 Ⓐ Ⓑ Ⓒ Ⓓ
3 Ⓐ Ⓑ Ⓒ Ⓓ	18 Ⓐ Ⓑ Ⓒ Ⓓ	33 Ⓐ Ⓑ Ⓒ Ⓓ	48 Ⓐ Ⓑ Ⓒ Ⓓ
4 Ⓐ Ⓑ Ⓒ Ⓓ	19 Ⓐ Ⓑ Ⓒ Ⓓ	34 Ⓐ Ⓑ Ⓒ Ⓓ	39 Ⓐ Ⓑ Ⓒ Ⓓ
5 Ⓐ Ⓑ Ⓒ Ⓓ	20 Ⓐ Ⓑ Ⓒ Ⓓ	35 Ⓐ Ⓑ Ⓒ Ⓓ	50 Ⓐ Ⓑ Ⓒ Ⓓ
6 Ⓐ Ⓑ Ⓒ Ⓓ	21 Ⓐ Ⓑ Ⓒ Ⓓ	36 Ⓐ Ⓑ Ⓒ Ⓓ	51 Ⓐ Ⓑ Ⓒ Ⓓ
7 Ⓐ Ⓑ Ⓒ Ⓓ	22 Ⓐ Ⓑ Ⓒ Ⓓ	37 Ⓐ Ⓑ Ⓒ Ⓓ	52 Ⓐ Ⓑ Ⓒ Ⓓ
8 Ⓐ Ⓑ Ⓒ Ⓓ	23 Ⓐ Ⓑ Ⓒ Ⓓ	38 Ⓐ Ⓑ Ⓒ Ⓓ	53 Ⓐ Ⓑ Ⓒ Ⓓ
9 Ⓐ Ⓑ Ⓒ Ⓓ	24 Ⓐ Ⓑ Ⓒ Ⓓ	39 Ⓐ Ⓑ Ⓒ Ⓓ	54 Ⓐ Ⓑ Ⓒ Ⓓ
10 Ⓐ Ⓑ Ⓒ Ⓓ	25 Ⓐ Ⓑ Ⓒ Ⓓ	40 Ⓐ Ⓑ Ⓒ Ⓓ	55 Ⓐ Ⓑ Ⓒ Ⓓ
11 Ⓐ Ⓑ Ⓒ Ⓓ	26 Ⓐ Ⓑ Ⓒ Ⓓ	41 Ⓐ Ⓑ Ⓒ Ⓓ	56 Ⓐ Ⓑ Ⓒ Ⓓ
12 Ⓐ Ⓑ Ⓒ Ⓓ	27 Ⓐ Ⓑ Ⓒ Ⓓ	42 Ⓐ Ⓑ Ⓒ Ⓓ	57 Ⓐ Ⓑ Ⓒ Ⓓ
13 Ⓐ Ⓑ Ⓒ Ⓓ	28 Ⓐ Ⓑ Ⓒ Ⓓ	43 Ⓐ Ⓑ Ⓒ Ⓓ	58 Ⓐ Ⓑ Ⓒ Ⓓ
14 Ⓐ Ⓑ Ⓒ Ⓓ	29 Ⓐ Ⓑ Ⓒ Ⓓ	44 Ⓐ Ⓑ Ⓒ Ⓓ	59 Ⓐ Ⓑ Ⓒ Ⓓ
15 Ⓐ Ⓑ Ⓒ Ⓓ	30 Ⓐ Ⓑ Ⓒ Ⓓ	45 Ⓐ Ⓑ Ⓒ Ⓓ	60 Ⓐ Ⓑ Ⓒ Ⓓ

2) If $m = 6$ and $n = -3$, what is the value of $\frac{5-9(3+n)}{3m-5(2-n)} = ?$

A. $\frac{2}{7}$

B. $\frac{3}{7}$

C. $-\frac{4}{7}$

D. $-\frac{5}{7}$

2) A child grows $1\frac{1}{7}$ inches in $\frac{1}{5}$ of a year. What would be his yearly growth rate in inches per year?

A. $\frac{2}{3}$

B. $5\frac{5}{7}$

C. $\frac{2}{3}$

D. $\frac{2}{3}$

3) The probability of drawing a blue candy at random from a bag of 30 candies is $\frac{3}{5}$. After 6 blue candies are removed from the bag, what is the probability of randomly drawing a blue candy from the bag?

A. $\frac{1}{2}$

B. $\frac{1}{4}$

C. $\frac{3}{5}$

D. 1

4) What is the greatest integer less than $-\frac{32}{5}$?

A. 0

B. -2

C. -4

D. -7

5) Kim earned $55 an hour. John earned 10% less than Kim. How much money did John earn in an hour?

   A. $43.50

   B. $45.50

   C. $47.50

   D. $49.50

6) In the figure below, a square is inscribed in a circle. Calculate the shaded area in the figure below. Knowing that the radius of the circle is $6\ cm$. ($\pi = 3.14$)

   A. $73.65\ cm^2$

   B. $69.90\ cm^2$

   C. $72.69\ cm^2$

   D. $88.04\ cm^2$

7) How many positive even factors of 68 are greater than 26 and less than 60?

   A. 0

   B. 1

   C. 2

   D. 6

8) In a box of blue and yellow pens, the ratio of yellow pens to blue pens is $2:3$. If the box contains 9 blue pens, how many yellow pens are there?

   A. 3

   B. 4

   C. 5

   D. 6

9) Find the value of x? $(2)^3 + (-3)^2 + 2x - 6 = 11$

   A. 0

   B. 2

   C. 4

   D. 6

10) In a certain state, the sales tax rate increased from 8% to 8.5%. What was the increase in the sales tax on a $250 item?

    A. $1.00

    B. $1.25

    C. $1.90

    D. $2.30

11) What decimal is equivalent to $-\frac{6}{9}$?

    A. $-0.\overline{5}$

    B. $-0.\overline{6}$

    C. $-0.\overline{65}$

    D. $-0.\overline{7}$

12) Sara has a box containing 5 blue balls, 8 red balls, and 3 green balls. If she removes one ball at random, what is the probability that it will not be blue?

    A. $\frac{5}{11}$

    B. $\frac{5}{16}$

    C. $\frac{10}{11}$

    D. $\frac{11}{16}$

13) In the figure below, $LMNO$ and $JMPQ$ are squares. Point O is the center of the circle, and points L and N are on the circle. If the area of the square is 16 square centimeters, what is the area, in square centimeters, of the shaded part? ($\pi = 3.14$)

    A. 3.14

    B. 3.44

    C. 4.55

    D. 5.46

14) Simplify the expression

$$(6x^3 - 8x^2 + 2x^4) - (4x^2 - 2x^4 + 2x^3)$$

A. $4x^3 - 12x^2$

B. $8x^3 - 12x^2$

C. $4x^4 + 4x^3 - 12x^2$

D. $4x^4 + 8x^3 - 12x^2$

15) $\frac{6}{11}$ of a number is 96. What is the number?

A. 97

B. 128

C. 154

D. 176

16) There are only red and blue cards in a box. The probability of choosing a red card in the box at random is one third. If there are 246 blue cards, how many cards are in the box?

A. 123

B. 308

C. 328

D. 369

17) Kim spent $35 for pants. This was $10 less than triple what she spent for a shirt. How much was the shirt?

A. $11

B. $13

C. $15

D. $17

18) If $5n$ is a positive even number, how many odd numbers are in the range from $5n$ up to and including $5n + 6$?

A. 2

B. 3

C. 4

D. 5

19) What are the zeros of the function: $f(x) = x^2 - 7x + 12$?

A. 0

B. $-2, -3$

C. $0, 4, 3$

D. $4, 3$

20) Which number line below shows the solution to the inequality $-1 < \frac{x}{3} < 2$?

A.

B.

C.

D.

21) How long will it take to receive \$360 in investment of \$240 at the rate of 10% simple interest?

A. 9 years

B. 15 years

C. 18 years

D. 21 years

22) Triangle ABC is graphed on a coordinate grid with vertices at $A(-3, -2), B(-1, 4)$ and $C(7, 9)$. Triangle ABC is reflected over x axes to create triangle $A'B'C'$. Which order pair represents the coordinate of C'?

A. $(7, 9)$

B. $(-7, -9)$

C. $(-7, 9)$

D. $(7, -9)$

23) If 150% of a number is 75, then what is the 90% of that number?

    A. 45

    B. 50

    C. 70

    D. 85

24) What is the slope of the line: $8x - 4y = 8$?

    A. -1

    B. -2

    C. 1

    D. 2

25) For what value of x is the proportion true? $x : 40 = 20 : 32$

    A. 16

    B. 25

    C. 28

    D. 32

26) $\frac{1}{6b^2} + \frac{1}{6b} = \frac{1}{b^2}$, then b = ?

    A. $-\frac{16}{15}$

    B. $-\frac{15}{16}$

    C. 5

    D. 8

27) Five years ago, Amy was three times as old as Mike was. If Mike is 10 years old now, how old is Amy?

    A. 4

    B. 8

    C. 12

    D. 20

28) If a tree casts a 18–foot shadow at the same time that a 4 feet yardstick casts a 3–foot shadow, what is the height of the tree?

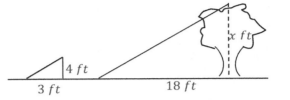

A. $18\ ft$

B. $20\ ft$

C. $24\ ft$

D. $54\ ft$

29) x is y% of what number?

A. $\dfrac{100x}{y}$

B. $\dfrac{100y}{x}$

C. $\dfrac{x}{100y}$

D. $\dfrac{y}{100x}$

30) If car A drives 600 miles in 8 hours and car B drives the same distance in 7.5 hours, how many miles per hour does car B drive faster than car A?

A. 80

B. 25

C. 10

D. 5

31) 6 liters of water are poured into an aquarium that's 15 cm long, 5 cm wide, and 60 cm high. How many cm will the water level in the aquarium rise due to this added water?

(1 liter of water = 1,000 cm^3)

A. 80

B. 40

C. 20

D. 10

32) If a box contains red and blue balls in ratio of $2:3$, how many red balls are there if 90 blue balls are in the box?

A. 90

B. 60

C. 30

D. 10

33) If $|a| < 1$, then which of the following is true? $(b > 0)$?

      I. $-b < ba < b$

      II. $-a < a^2 < a \quad if \ a < 0$

      III. $-5 < 2a - 3 < -1$

A. I only

B. II only

C. I and III only

D. III only

34) Which graph shows a non-proportional linear relationship between x and y?

A.

B.

C.

D.

35) If 30% of a number is 12, what is the number?

A. 12

B. 25

C. 40

D. 45

36) A car travels at a speed of 72 miles per hour. How far will it travel in 8 hours?

    A. 574 miles

    B. 576 miles

    C. 578 miles

    D. 580 miles

37) Four straight lines interest at point O as shown below. What is the value of x?

    A. $20°$

    B. $25°$

    C. $30°$

    D. $35°$

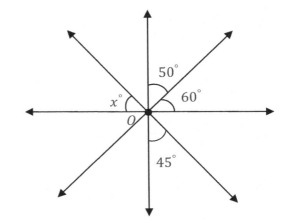

38) The following table represents the value of x and function $f(x)$. Which of the following could be the equation of the function $f(x)$?

    A. $f(x) = x^2 - 5$

    B. $f(x) = x^2 - 1$

    C. $f(x) = \sqrt{x + 2}$

    D. $f(x) = \sqrt{x} + 4$

x	$f(x)$
1	5
4	6
9	7
16	8

39) In the following equation when z is divided by 3, what is the effect on x?

$$x = \frac{8y + \dfrac{r}{r+1}}{\dfrac{6}{z}}$$

    A. x is divided by 2

    B. x is divided by 3

    C. x does not change

    D. x is multiplied by 3

40) The greatest common factor of 32 and x is 8. How many possible values for x are greater than 10 and less than 60?

A. 1

B. 4

C. 6

D. 7

41) If x is a real number, and if $x^3 + 18 = 130$, then x lies between which two consecutive integers?

A. 1 and 2

B. 2 and 3

C. 3 and 4

D. 4 and 5

42) If $\frac{3x}{25} = \frac{x-1}{5}$, $x =$

A. $\frac{1}{5}$

B. $\frac{5}{2}$

C. 3

D. 5

43) If $(x - 2)^3 = 27$ which of the following could be the value of $(x - 6)(x - 4)$?

A. 1

B. -1

C. 2

D. 6

44) 120 is equal to

A. $20 - (4 \times 10) + (6 \times 30)$

B. $\left(\frac{11}{8} \times 72\right) + \left(\frac{125}{5}\right)$

C. $\left(\left(\frac{30}{4} + \frac{13}{2}\right) \times 7\right) - \frac{11}{2} + \frac{110}{4}$

D. $(2 \times 10) + (50 \times 1.5) + 15$

45) What is the length of AB in the following figure if $AE = 4, CD = 6$ and $AC = 12$?

A. 3.8

B. 4.8

C. 7.2

D. 24

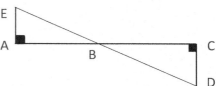

46) In the following figure, MN is $40\ cm$. How long is ON?

A. $10\ cm$

B. $15\ cm$

C. $20\ cm$

D. $25\ cm$

47) What is the value of the following expression? $|-5| + 9 \times 2\frac{1}{3} + (-3)^2 =$

A. 26

B. 35

C. 43

D. 51

48) What are the zeroes of the function $f(x) = x^3 + 8x^2 + 12x$?

A. 2

B. 6

C. $0, 2, 6$

D. $0, -2, -6$

49) If the area of the following rectangular $ABCD$ is 100, and E is the midpoint of AB, what is the area of the shaded part

A. 25

B. 45

C. 50

D. 80

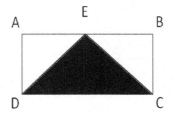

50) In the figure below, F is the midpoint of EH. Which segment has length $2y - x$ centimeters?

A. EF

B. GH

C. EG

D. FH

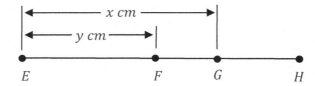

51) The function $g(x)$ is defined by a polynomial. Some values of x and $g(x)$ are shown in the table below. Which of the following must be a factor of $g(x)$?

x	$g(x)$
-1	4
-2	0
0	5
1	4
2	6

    A. $x - 2$

    B. $x - 1$

    C. $x + 2$

    D. $x + 1$

52) Divide: $\frac{16n^6 - 32n^2 + 8n}{8n}$

    A. $2n^5 - 4n$

    B. $2n^6 - 4n^2$

    C. $2n^5 - 4n + 1$

    D. $2n^6 - 4n^2 + 1$

53) $\frac{1\frac{4}{3} + \frac{1}{4}}{2\frac{1}{2} - \frac{17}{8}}$ is approximately equal to

    A. 5.88

    B. 6.88

    C. 9

    D. 12

54) Which is the correct statement?

    A. $\frac{3}{4} > 0.8$

    B. $10\% = \frac{2}{5}$

    C. $3 < \frac{5}{2}$

    D. $\frac{5}{6} > 0.8$

55) Simplify: $\frac{\left(\frac{40(x+1)}{4}\right) - 10}{12}$

    A. $\frac{3}{7}x$

    B. $\frac{5}{6}x$

    C. $\frac{5}{12}x$

    D. $\frac{12}{5}x$

56) When 40% of 60 is added to 12% of 600, the resulting number is:

A. 24

B. 72

C. 96

D. 140

57) If $f(x) = 7x - 5$ and $g(x) = 2x^2 - 4x$, then find $(\frac{f}{g})(x)$.

A. $\frac{7x-5}{2x^2-4x}$

B. $\frac{x-1}{x^2-1}$

C. $\frac{7x-1}{x^2-2}$

D. $\frac{7x+5}{x^2+2x}$

58) Which of the following is the solution of the following inequality?
$$2x + 4 > 11x - 12.5 - 3.5x$$

A. $x < 3$

B. $x > 3$

C. $x \leq 4$

D. $x \geq 4$

59) Let r and p be constants. If $x^2 + 6x + r$ factors into $(x + 2)(x + p)$, the values of r and p respectively are?

A. 8 , 4

B. 4 , 8

C. 6 , 3

D. 3 , 6

60) Which of the following expressions is equal to $\sqrt{\frac{x^2}{2} + \frac{x^2}{16}}$?

A. x

B. $\frac{3x}{4}$

C. $x\sqrt{x}$

D. $\frac{x\sqrt{x}}{4}$

End of CLEP College Mathematics Practice Test 2

CLEP College Math Practice Tests Answer Keys

Now, it's time to review your results to see where you went wrong and what areas you need to improve.

CLEP College Mathematics Practice Test 1						CLEP College Mathematics Practice Test 2					
1	D	21	B	41	C	1	D	21	B	41	D
2	D	22	D	42	B	2	B	22	D	42	B
3	D	23	C	43	B	3	A	23	A	43	B
4	B	24	D	44	A	4	D	24	D	44	C
5	D	25	B	45	C	5	D	25	B	45	B
6	A	26	A	46	D	6	D	26	C	46	D
7	C	27	D	47	D	7	B	27	D	47	B
8	B	28	B	48	D	8	D	28	C	48	D
9	C	29	C	49	D	9	A	29	A	49	C
10	C	30	C	50	C	10	B	30	D	50	B
11	D	31	B	51	B	11	B	31	A	51	C
12	D	32	C	52	C	12	D	32	B	52	C
13	D	33	D	53	B	13	B	33	C	53	B
14	C	34	C	54	D	14	C	34	C	54	D
15	B	35	C	55	C	15	D	35	C	55	B
16	A	36	A	56	A	16	D	36	B	56	C
17	C	37	D	57	A	17	C	37	B	57	A
18	D	38	D	58	D	18	B	38	D	58	A
19	D	39	C	59	D	19	D	39	B	59	A
20	A	40	A	60	A	20	D	40	B	60	B

CLEP College Mathematics Practice Tests Answers and Explanations

CLEP College Mathematics Practice Test 1

Answers and Explanations

1) Choice D is correct

$g(x) = -2$, then $f(g(x)) = f(-2) = 3(-2)^3 + 5(-2)^2 + 2(-2) = -24 + 20 - 4 = -8$

2) Choice D is correct

To answer this question, add $\frac{2}{7}$ and $\frac{3}{8}$: $\frac{2}{7} + \frac{3}{8} = \frac{16+21}{56} = \frac{37}{56} \, ml$

3) Choice D is correct

$x = \frac{1}{3}$ and $y = \frac{9}{21}$, substitute the values of x and y in the expression and simplify:

$\frac{1}{x} \div \frac{y}{3} \rightarrow \frac{1}{\frac{1}{3}} \div \frac{\frac{9}{21}}{3} \rightarrow \frac{1}{\frac{1}{3}} = 3$ and $\frac{\frac{9}{21}}{3} = \frac{9}{63} = \frac{1}{7}$. Then: $\frac{1}{\frac{1}{3}} \div \frac{\frac{9}{21}}{3} = 3 \div \frac{1}{7} = 3 \times 7 = 21$

4) Choice B is correct

The original piece of paper is $2\frac{3}{5}$ feet long.

The shorter piece is x feet long, and it must be less than half the length of the original piece of paper. Since half of $2\frac{3}{5}$ is $1\frac{3}{10}$ it follows that $x < 1\frac{3}{10}$.

5) Choice D is correct

Solve for x. $-4 \le 4x - 8 < 16 \Rightarrow$ (add 8 all sides) $-4 + 8 \le 4x - 8 + 8 < 16 + 8 \Rightarrow$

$4 \le 4x < 24 \Rightarrow$ (divide all sides by 4) $1 \le x < 6$. x is between 1 and 6. Choice D represents this inequality.

6) Choice A is correct

First, find the sale price. 15% of $45.00 is $6.75, so the sale price is $45.00 - $6.75 = $38.25
Next, find the price after Nick's employee discount. $20\% \times \$38.25 = \$7.65$, so, the final price of the shoes is $38.25 - $7.65 = $30.60

7) Choice C is correct

To find the number of possible outfit combinations, multiply number of options for each factor:

$3 \times 7 \times 4 = 84$

8) Choice B is correct

Volume of the cube is less than $64 \, m^3$. Use the formula of volume of cubes.

Volume $= (one \, side)^3 \Rightarrow 64 = (one \, side)^3$. Find the cube root of both sides.

$64 = (one \, side)^3 \rightarrow one \, side = \sqrt[3]{64} = 4$

Then: $4 =$ one side. The side of the cube is less than 4. Only choice A is less than 4.

9) Choice C is correct

There are 60 minutes in 1 hours. Divide the number of minutes by the number of minutes in 1 hour: $\frac{1,800}{60} = 30$ hours

10) Choice C is correct

Use the average formula: average (mean) $= \frac{sum\ of\ terms}{number\ of\ terms} = \frac{9+12+15+16+19+16+14.5}{7} = 14.5$

11) Choice D is correct

Jack scored a mean of 80 per test. In the first 4 tests, the sum of scores is: $80 \times 4 = 320$. Now, calculate the mean over the 5 tests: $\frac{320+90}{5} = \frac{410}{5} = 82$

12) Choice D is correct

Th ratio of boy to girls is $4:7$. Therefore, there are 4 boys out of 11 students. To find the answer, first divide the total number of students by 11, then multiply the result by 4.

$66 \div 11 = 6 \Rightarrow 6 \times 4 = 24$, There are 24 boys and $42 = (66 - 24)$ girls. So, 18 more boys should be enrolled to make the ratio $1:1$.

13) Choice D is correct

The amount of money that Jack earns for one hour: $\frac{\$616}{44} = \$14$

A number of additional hours that he works to make enough money is: $\frac{\$826-\$616}{1.5\times\$14} = 10$

Number of total hours is: $44 + 10 = 54$

14) Choice C is correct

The first integer is m, so the second is $m + 1$, the rest are $m + 2, m + 3, m + 4, m + 5, m + 6$ and finally $m + 7$. Since n is the eight and greatest of the integers, $n = m + 7$

Substitute $m + 7$ for n and simplify: $\frac{m+n}{3} = \frac{m+m+7}{3} = \frac{2m+7}{3}$

15) Choice B is correct

Use simple interest formula: $I = prt$ ($I = interest, p = principal, r = rate, t = time$)

$I = prt \rightarrow 600 = (3,000)(0.05)(t) \rightarrow 600 = 150t \rightarrow t = 4$

16) Choice A is correct

Simplify and combine like terms.

$(5x^3 - 8x^2 + 2x^4) - (4x^2 - 2x^4 + 2x^3) \Rightarrow 5x^3 - 8x^2 + 2x^4 - 4x^2 + 2x^4 - 2x^3 \Rightarrow 4x^4 + 3x^3 - 12x^2$

17) Choice C is correct

Since 90 boxes contain $360\ kg$ vegetable. Therefore, 1 box contains $\frac{360\ kg}{90} = 4\ kg$ vegetable.

18) Choice D is correct

One gram is equal to 1,000 milligrams, or 1 milligram is equal to $\frac{1}{1,000}$ gram

Thus, 85 milligrams $= \frac{85}{1,000} = 0.085$ gram

19) Choice D is correct

First, convert their heights from feet and inches to inches, by multiplying the number of feet by 12 and adding the inches. Tomas: 6 feet +8.5 inches. 6(12 inches) +8.5 inches= 72 inches +8.5 inches = 80.5 inches. Alex: 5 feet +3 inches. 5(12 inches)+3 inches = 60 inches + 3 inches = 63 inches

Then, subtract Alex's height from Tomas's height: $80.5 - 63 = 17.5$

20) Choice A is correct

First, find the sum of course grade of Anna, $average = \frac{sum\ of\ terms}{number\ of\ terms} \Rightarrow$

$80 = \dfrac{sum\ of\ course\ grade}{5} \rightarrow the\ sum\ of\ course\ grade = 80 \times 5 = 400$

Anna and William have the same sum of course grade, now find the Williams mean

$average = \dfrac{sum\ of\ course\ grade}{number\ of\ course} \Rightarrow \dfrac{400}{8} = 50$

21) Choice B is correct

Use the percent increase expression to find the answer:

$\dfrac{new\ price - original\ price}{original\ price} = \dfrac{5.67 - 5.40}{5.40} = 0.05 = 5\%$

22) Choice D is correct

The sum of the scores of Scarlett's 5 games is $5(159) = 795$. The sum of the scores of Marys' 3 games is $3(95) = 285$. Add those two sums and divide by 8 to find the mean:

$\dfrac{795 + 285}{8} = \dfrac{1,080}{8} = 135$

23) Choice C is correct

First draw an isosceles triangle. Remember that two legs of the triangle are equal.

Let put a for the legs. Then:

$a = 6 \Rightarrow$ Area of the triangle is $= \frac{1}{2}(6 \times 6) = \frac{36}{2} = 18\ cm^2$

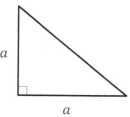

24) Choice D is correct

The equation of a line is in the form of $y = mx + b$, where m is the slope of the line and b is the $y - intercept$ of the line. Two points (4,3) and (3,2) are on line A. Therefore, the slope of the line A is: $slope\ of\ line\ A = \frac{y_2 - y_1}{x_2 - x_1} = \frac{2-3}{3-4} = \frac{-1}{-1} = 1$. The slope of line A is 1. Thus, the formula of the line A is: $y = mx + b = x + b$, choose a point and plug in the values of x and y in the equation to solve for b. Let's choose point (4, 3). Then: $y = x + b \rightarrow 3 = 4 + b \rightarrow b = 3 - 4 = -1$

The equation of line A is: $y = x - 1$. Now, let's review the choices provided:

A. $(-1, 2)$ $\quad\quad y = x - 1 \rightarrow 2 = -1 - 1 = -2$ This is not true.

B. $(5, 7)$ $\quad\quad y = x - 1 \rightarrow 7 = 5 - 1 = 4$ This is not true.

C. $(3, 4)$ $\quad\quad y = x - 1 \rightarrow 4 = 3 - 1 = 2$ This is not true.

D. $(-1, -2)$ $\quad y = x - 1 \rightarrow -2 = -1 - 1 = -2$ This is true!

25) Choice B is correct

First, change the improper fractions into mixed numbers: $\frac{7}{2} = 3\frac{1}{2}$ and $\frac{30}{4} = 7\frac{1}{2}$

The integers between these two values are $4, 5, 6$ and 7. So, there are 4 integers between $\frac{7}{5}$ and $\frac{30}{4}$.

26) Choice A is correct

The area of the entire circle is πr^2. The fraction of the circle that is shaded is $\frac{30}{360} = \frac{1}{12}$. So, the area of the sector is $\frac{1}{12}\pi r^2$. Use that information to find r.

$\frac{1}{12}\pi r^2 = 12\pi \rightarrow r^2 = 144 \rightarrow r = 12$

Use r to calculate the circumference of the circle: $c = 2\pi r = 2\pi(12) = 24\pi$

The circumference is 24π feet.

27) Choice D is correct

Based on triangle similarity theorem, set up a proportion to solve for x:

$\frac{x+8}{x} = \frac{6}{4} \rightarrow 4(x + 8) = 6x \rightarrow 4x + 32 = 6x \rightarrow 32 = 2x \rightarrow x = 16$

28) Choice B is correct

The factors of 45 are: $\{1, 3, 5, 9, 15, 45\}$. Only choice B is correct.

29) Choice C is correct

$ON = 4 - (-6) = 10$ units. Let $x = OM$. Then $MN = 10 - x$. Substitute these expressions in the given equation: $x = \frac{1}{3}(10 - x)$

Solve for x: $x = \frac{10}{3} - \frac{x}{3} \rightarrow x + \frac{x}{3} = \frac{10}{3} \rightarrow \frac{4x}{3} = \frac{10}{3} \rightarrow 4x = 10 \rightarrow x = \frac{10}{4} = \frac{5}{2} = 2.5$

$x = OM$. Point O is at -6. Then, point M is at: $-6 + 2.5 = -3.5$

30) Choice C is correct

Standard form of straight-line equation is: $y = mx + b$. Thus, choice C has a graph that is a straight line. All other options are not equations of straight lines.

31) Choice B is correct

Convert mixed number to fractions: $8\frac{4}{7} \times 2\frac{2}{3} = \frac{60}{7} \times \frac{8}{3}$, Multiply the numerators and denominators: $\frac{480}{21}$, Simplify the fraction: $\frac{480}{21} = \frac{160}{7}$, Convert to mixed numbers: $\frac{160}{7} = 22\frac{6}{7}$

32) Choice C is correct

Answer this question, divide $12\ km$ by $3\ km$ per hour: $\frac{12}{3} = 4$ hours

33) Choice D is correct

So far, Kylie has written $10\% + 18\% = 28\%$ of the entire homework. That means she has $100\% - 28\% = 72\%$ left to write. $72\% = \frac{72}{100} = \frac{18}{25}$

34) Choice C is correct

A zero of a function corresponds to an x-intercept of the graph of the function in the xy-plane. Therefore, the graph of the function $g(x)$, which has three distinct zeros, must have three $x-$intercepts. Only the graph in choice C has three $x-$intercepts.

35) Choice C is correct

The area of the trapezoid is:

Area$= \frac{1}{2} h(b_1 + b_2) = \frac{1}{2}(x)(13 + 8) = 126 \rightarrow 10.5x = 126 \rightarrow x = 12$

$y = \sqrt{5^2 + 12^2} = \sqrt{25 + 144} = \sqrt{169} = 13$

The perimeter of the trapezoid is: $12 + 13 + 8 + 13 = 46$

36) Choice A is correct

There are **12** sticks in the box $(\mathbf{6 + 4 + 2})$. So, the probability that Emma picks a green stick is:

Probability $= \frac{6}{12} = \frac{1}{2}$

37) Choice D is correct

Check each choice provided:

A. 1 $\quad \frac{4+5+8+11+12}{5} = \frac{40}{5} = 8$

B. 4 $\quad \frac{1+5+8+11+12}{5} = \frac{37}{5} = 7.4$

C. 5 $\quad \frac{1+4+8+11+12}{5} = \frac{36}{5} = 7.2$

D. 11 $\frac{1+4+5+8+12}{5} = \frac{30}{5} = 6$

38) Choice D is correct

The capacity of a red box is 20% bigger than the capacity of a blue box and it can hold 60 books. Therefore, we want to find a number that 20% bigger than that number is 60. Let x be that number. Then: $1.20 \times x = 60$, Divide both sides of the equation by 1.2. Then:

$x = \frac{60}{1.20} = 50$

39) Choice C is correct

Plug in the value of each choice in the inequality.

A. 1 $(1 - 2)^2 + 1 > 3(1) - 1 \rightarrow 2 > 2$ This is Not true

B. 6 $(6-2)^2 + 1 > 3(6) - 1 \rightarrow 17 > 17$ This is Not true

C. 8 $(8-2)^2 + 1 > 3(8) - 1 \rightarrow 37 > 23$ This is true

D. 3 $(3-2)^2 + 1 > 3(3) - 1 \rightarrow 2 > 8$ This is Not true

40) Choice A is correct

The relationship among all sides of right triangle $30° - 60° - 90°$ is provided

in the following triangle: Sine of $30°$ equals to: $\frac{opposite}{hypotenuse} = \frac{x}{2x} = \frac{1}{2}$

41) Choice C is correct

Solve for x: $0.00104 = \frac{104}{x}$, multiply both sides by x, $(0.00104)(x) = \frac{104}{x}(x)$.

Simplify: $0.00104x = 104$. Divide both side by 0.00104: $\frac{0.00104x}{0.00104} = \frac{104}{0.00104}$, simplify

$$x = \frac{104}{0.00104} = 100,000$$

42) Choice B is correct

Multiply two exponents: $(x^6)^{\frac{7}{8}} = x^{6 \times \frac{7}{8}} = x^{\frac{42}{8}} = x^{\frac{21}{4}}$

43) Choice B is correct

$\frac{x}{5} = \frac{y-x}{4} \rightarrow 4x = 5y - 5x \rightarrow 5y = 9x \rightarrow y = \frac{9}{5}x$

44) Choice A is correct

Let the lengths of two sides of the parallelogram be $2x\ cm$ and $3x\ cm$ respectively. Then, its perimeter $= 2(2x + 3x) = 10x$

Therefore, $10x = 40 \rightarrow x = 4$

One side $= 2(4) = 8\ cm$ and other side is: $3(4) = 12\ cm$

45) Choice C is correct

Use properties of equations to determine the missing expression. $\frac{2y}{x} - \frac{y}{3x} = \frac{(\ldots)}{3x}$

$\frac{3}{3} \cdot \frac{2y}{x} - \frac{y}{3x} = \frac{(\ldots)}{3x} \rightarrow \frac{6y}{3x} - \frac{y}{3x} = \frac{(\ldots)}{3x} \rightarrow \frac{6y-y}{3x} = \frac{(\ldots)}{3x} \rightarrow (\ldots) = 5y$

46) Choice D is correct

Let E age of Ella, we know Ella is 4 years older than Ava: $E = 4 + A \rightarrow A = S - 3$

47) Choice D is correct

If x is the smaller consecutive integer, then $x + 1$ is the larger consecutive integer. Use their sum (-13) to find x: $x + (x + 1) = -13 \rightarrow 2x + 1 = -13 \rightarrow 2x = -14 \rightarrow x = -7$

The two consecutive integers are -7 and -6. 2 is added to the smaller integer: $-7 + 2 = -5$, and 3 is subtracted from the larger integer: $-6 - 3 = -9$ find the product: $-5 \times (-9) = 45$

48) Choice D is correct

The problem asks for the sum of the roots of the quadratic equation $2n^2 + 16n + 24 = 0$. Dividing each side of the equation by 2 gives $n^2 + 8n + 12 = 0$. If the roots of

$n^2 + 8n + 12 = 0$ are n_1 and n_2, then the equation can be factored as

$n^2 + 8n + 12 = (n - n_1)(n - n_2) = 0$. Looking at the coefficient of n on each side of

$n^2 + 8n + 12 = (n + 6)(n + 2)$ gives $n = -6$ or $n = -2$,   then, $-6 + (-2) = -8$

49) Choice D is correct

Length of the rectangle is: $\frac{4}{5} \times 30 = 24$, Perimeter of rectangle is: $2 \times (24 + 30) = 108$

50) Choice C is correct

There are 6 spaces, so first divide 140 by 6: $140 \div 6 = 23$ remainder 2. So, the arrow goes around 23 full circle and then 2 more spaces. Two spaces from Space O is Space Q.

51) Choice B is correct

Plug in 25 for x in the equation.

A. $x + 10 = 40 \rightarrow 25 + 10 \neq 40$

B. $4x = 100 \rightarrow 4(25) = 100$

C. $3x = 70 \rightarrow 3(25) \neq 70$

D. $\frac{x}{2} = 12 \rightarrow \frac{25}{2} \neq 12$

Only choice B is correct.

52) Choice C is correct

Use the values of x and y from the chart to graph the line. Choice B represents the chart.

53) Choice B is correct

Simplify the numerator: $\frac{x + (5x)^2 + (3x)^3}{x} = \frac{x + 5^2x^2 + 3^3x^3}{x} = \frac{x + 25x^2 + 27x^3}{x}$

Pull an x out of each term in the numerator. $\frac{x(1 + 25x + 27x^2)}{x}$

The x in the numerator and the x in the denominator cancel:

$1 + 25x + 27x^2 = 27x^2 + 25x + 1$

54) Choice D is correct

Since the triangle ABC is reflected over the y-axis, then all values of y's of the points don't change and the sign of all x's change. (remember that when a point is reflected over the y-axis, the value of y does not change and when a point is reflected over the x-axis, the value of x does not change). Therefore: $(-1,6)$ changes to $(1,6)$. $(-2,5)$ changes to $(2,5)$. $(5,8)$ changes to $(-5,8)$

55) Choice C is correct

The area of rectangle is: $9 \times 4 = 36 \ cm^2$.

The area of circle is: $\pi r^2 = \pi \times (\frac{10}{2})^2 = 3 \times 25 = 75 \ cm^2$.

Difference of areas is: $75 - 36 = 39$

56) Choice A is correct

$x - 2 \geq 3 \to x \geq 3 + 2 \to x \geq 5.$ Or $x - 2 \leq -3 \to x \leq -3 + 2 \to x \leq -1$

Then, solution is: $x \geq 5 \cup x \leq -1$

57) Choice A is correct

The easiest way to solve this one is to plug the answers into the equation.

When you do this, you will see the only time $x = x^{-6}$ is when $x = 1$ or $x = 0$.

Only $x = 1$ is provided in the choices.

58) Choice D is correct

Based on triangle similarity theorem: $\frac{a}{a+b} = \frac{c}{3} \to c = \frac{3a}{a+b} = \frac{3\sqrt{3}}{3\sqrt{3}} = 1 \to$

area of shaded region is: $\left(\frac{c+3}{2}\right)(b) = \frac{4}{2} \times 2\sqrt{3} = 4\sqrt{3}$

59) Choice D is correct

The angle $(2x - 5)$ and 55 are supplementary angles. Therefore:

$(2x - 5) + 55 = 180 \to 2x + 50 = 180 \to 2x = 180 - 50 = 130 \to x = \dfrac{130}{2} \to x = 65$

60) Choice A is correct

Let y be Anna's age. Then:

$5y + 3 = x \to 5y = x - 3 \to y = \frac{x-3}{5}$

CLEP College Mathematics Practice Test 2

Answers and Explanations

1) Choice D is correct

Substitute 6 for m and -3 for n:

$\frac{5-9(3+n)}{3m-5(2-n)} = \frac{5-9(3+(-3))}{3(6)-5(2-(-3))} = \frac{5-9(0)}{18-5(5)} = \frac{5}{18-25} = \frac{5}{-7} = -\frac{5}{7}$

2) Choice B is correct

Set up a proportion to solve.

$\frac{1\frac{1}{7} in}{\frac{1}{5} yr} = \frac{x \, in}{1 \, yr} \rightarrow 1\frac{1}{7} = \frac{1}{5}x \rightarrow \frac{8}{7} = \frac{1}{5}x \rightarrow \left(\frac{5}{1}\right)\left(\frac{8}{7}\right) = x \rightarrow \frac{40}{7} = x \rightarrow x = 5\frac{5}{7}$

3) Choice A is correct

Start with a proportion to determine the total number of blue candies in the bag.

$\frac{3}{5} = \frac{r}{30} \rightarrow \frac{3}{5}(30) = r \rightarrow r = 18$

There are currently 18 blue candies out of 30 candies in the bag. After 6 blue candies are removed, there would be 12 blue candies left in the bag and 24 total candies.

The probability of randomly drawing a blue candy would then be $\frac{12}{24} = \frac{1}{2}$

4) Choice D is correct

First, convert the improper fraction to a mixed number: $-\frac{32}{5} = -6\frac{2}{5}$

The two closest integers to this fraction are -7 and -6. The integer less than $-\frac{32}{5}$ is -7.

5) Choice D is correct

If Kim's earning $= 100\%$, then, John's earning is 90% of Kim's earning. Then:

$0.90 \times 55 = 49.50$

6) Choice D is correct

First, calculate the area of the circle and the area of the square:

Area of the circle $= \pi r^2 = \pi(6)^2 = 36\pi = 113.04 \, cm^2$

Area of the square $= 5 \, cm \times 5 \, cm = 25 \, cm^2$

To calculate the shaded area, subtract the area of the square from the area of the circle:

$113.04 \, cm^2 - 25 \, cm^2 = 88.04 \, cm^2$

7) Choice B is correct

List the factors of 68: 1 and 68, 2 and 34, 4 and 17. There is one factor greater than 26 and less than 60.

8) Choice D is correct

Let x be the number of yellow pens. Write a proportion and solve: $\frac{yellow}{blue} = \frac{2}{3} = \frac{x}{9}$

Solve the equation: $18 = 3x \rightarrow x = 6$

9) Choice A is correct

$(2)^3 + (-3)^2 + 2x - 6 = 11 \rightarrow 8 + 9 + 2x - 6 = 11$

174

Combine like terms: $11 + 2x = 11 \rightarrow 2x = 0 \rightarrow x = 0$

10) Choice B is correct

The increase in sales tax percentage is $8.5\% - 8.0\% = 0.5\%$

0.5% of $\$250$ is $(0.5\%)(250) = (0.005)(250) = 1.25\$$

11) Choice B is correct

To find the decimal equivalent to $-\frac{6}{9}$, divide 6 by 9. Then:

$$-\frac{6}{9} = -0.66666\ldots = -0.\overline{6}$$

12) Choice D is correct

There are currently 16 balls in the bag $(5 + 8 + 3)$. Of those balls, 11 are not blue. So, the probability of choosing a ball that is not blue is $\frac{11}{16}$.

13) Choice B is correct

The area of square $LMNO$ is 16 square centimeters. So: $S^2 = 16 \rightarrow \sqrt{S^2} = \sqrt{16} \rightarrow S = 4\ cm$

Sides LO and NO are each a radius of the circle. So, the radius of the circle is $4\ cm$.

calculate the area of $\frac{1}{4}$ of the circle. The area of a circle is $A = \pi r^2$. So the area of the $\frac{1}{4}$ of the circle, in square centimeters is $\frac{1}{4}A = \frac{1}{4}\pi r^2 = \frac{1}{4}\pi(4)^2 = \frac{1}{4}\pi(16) = 4\pi$. For calculating the area of shaded region, subtract area of $\frac{1}{4}$ of the circle from area of square.

The area of the shaded par: $16 - 4\pi$: and $\pi = 3.14$, then, the answer is:

$16 - 4\pi = 16 - 12.56 = 3.44$

14) Choice C is correct

$(6x^3 - 8x^2 + 2x^4) - (4x^2 - 2x^4 + 2x^3) = (6x^3 - 8x^2 + 2x^4) - 4x^2 + 2x^4 - 2x^3 =$

$4x^4 + 4x^3 - 12x^2$

15) Choice D is correct

Let x be the number: $\frac{6}{11}x = 96 \rightarrow x = 96 \times \frac{11}{6} = 176$

16) Choice D is correct

Let x be total number of cards in the box, then number of red cards is: $x - 246$

The probability of choosing a red card is one third. Then: $probability = \frac{1}{3} = \frac{x-132}{x}$

Use cross multiplication to solve for $x. =$

$x \times 1 = 3(x - 246) \rightarrow x = 3x - 738 \rightarrow 2x = 738 \rightarrow x = 369$

17) Choice C is correct

Convert everything into an equation: $35 = (3 \times shirt) - 10$

Now, solve the equation: $45 = 3$ shirt $\rightarrow$ shirt $= \frac{45}{3} = 15$.

18) Choice B is correct

Since $5n$ is even, then $5n + 1$ must be odd. Thus $5n + 3$ and $5n + 5$ are also odd. So, there are a total of 3 numbers in this range that are odd.

19) Choice D is correct

First factor the function: $(x - 4)(x - 3)$. To find the zeros, $f(x)$ should be zero: $f(x) = (x - 4)(x - 3) = 0$,Therefore, the zeros are, $(x - 4) = 0 \Rightarrow x = 4$, $(x - 3) = 0 \Rightarrow x = 3$

20) Choice D is correct

Multiply each term by 3 to eliminate the fraction, and isolate x:

$-1(3) < \left(\frac{x}{3}\right)(3) < 2(3) \rightarrow -3 < x < 6$, therefore, x must be between -3 and 6. Only Choice D represents all values of x.

21) Choice B is correct

Simple interest (y) is calculated by multiplying the initial deposit (p), by the interest rate (r), and time (t). $360 = 240 \times 0.10 \times t \rightarrow 360 = 24t \rightarrow t = \frac{360}{24} = 15$

So, it takes 15 years to get \$360 with an investment of \$240.

22) Choice D is correct

When a point is reflected over x axes, the (y) coordinate of that point changes to $(-y)$ while its x coordinate remains the same. $C(7, 9) \rightarrow C'(7, -9)$

23) Choice A is correct

First, find the number. Let x be the number. Write the equation and solve for x.

150% of a number is 75, then: $1.5 \times x = 75 \Rightarrow x = 75 \div 1.5 = 50$. 90% of 50 is:

$0.9 \times 50 = 45$

24) Choice D is correct

Solve for y: $8x - 4y = 8$, Divided both sides by -4: $\frac{8}{-4}x - \frac{4}{-4}y = \frac{8}{-4}$

$-2x + y = -2 \rightarrow y = 2x - 2$, Then: The slope of the line is 2.

25) Choice B is correct

Write the ratios in fraction form and solve for x: $\frac{x}{40} = \frac{20}{32}$

Cross multiply: $32x = 800$. Apply the multiplicative inverse property; divide both sides by 32:

$x = \frac{800}{32} = 25$

26) Choice C is correct

Subtract $\frac{1}{6b}$ and $\frac{1}{b^2}$ from both sides of the equation. Then:

$\frac{1}{6b^2} + \frac{1}{6b} = \frac{1}{b^2} \rightarrow \frac{1}{6b^2} - \frac{1}{b^2} = -\frac{1}{6b}$

176

Multiply both numerator and denominator of the fraction $\frac{1}{b^2}$ by 6. Then:

$$\frac{1}{6b^2} - \frac{6}{6b^2} = -\frac{1}{6b}$$

Simplify the first side of the equation: $-\frac{5}{6b^2} = -\frac{1}{6b}$

Use cross multiplication method: $30b = 6b^2 \rightarrow 30 = 6b \rightarrow b = 5$

27) Choice D is correct

Five years ago, Amy was three times as old as Mike. Mike is 10 years now. Therefore, 5 years ago Mike was 5 years. Five years ago, Amy was: $A = 3 \times 5 = 15$, Now Amy is 20 years old:

$$15 + 5 = 20$$

28) Choice C is correct

Write a proportion and solve for x: $\frac{4}{3} = \frac{x}{18} \Rightarrow 3x = 18 \times 4 \Rightarrow x = \frac{72}{3} = 24\ ft$

29) Choice A is correct

Let the number be A. Then: $x = y\% \times A$. Solve for A. $x = \frac{y}{100} \times A$

Multiply both sides by $\frac{100}{y}$: $x \times \frac{100}{y} = \frac{y}{100} \times \frac{100}{y} \times A \rightarrow A = \frac{100x}{y}$

30) Choice D is correct

Speed of car A is: $\frac{600}{8} = 75\ \frac{km}{h}$, Speed of car B is: $\frac{600}{7.5} = 80\ \frac{km}{h}$, $\rightarrow 80 - 75 = 5\ \frac{km}{h}$

31) Choice A is correct

One liter $= 1{,}000\ cm^3 \rightarrow$ 6 liters$= 6{,}000\ cm^3$

$$6{,}000 = 15 \times 5 \times h \rightarrow h = \frac{6{,}000}{75} = 80\ cm$$

32) Choice B is correct

$$\frac{2}{3} \times 90 = 60$$

33) Choice C is correct

I. $|a| < 1 \rightarrow -1 < a < 1$

Multiply all sides by b. Since, $b > 0 \rightarrow -b < ba < b$ (it is true!)

II. Since, $-1 < a < 1, and\ a < 0 \rightarrow -a > a^2 > a$ (plug in $-\frac{1}{2}$, and check!) (It's false)

III. $-1 < a < 1$,multiply all sides by 2, then: $-2 < 2a < 2$

Subtract 3 from all sides. Then: $-2 - 3 < 2a - 3 < 2 - 3 \rightarrow -5 < 2a - 3 < -1$ (It is true!)

34) Choice C is correct

A linear equation is a relationship between two variables, x and y, and can be written in the form of $y = mx + b$. A non-proportional linear relationship takes on the form $y = mx + b$, where

$b \neq 0$ and its graph is a line that does not cross through the origin. Only in graph C, the line does not pass through the origin.

35) Choice C is correct

Let x be the number. Write the equation and solve for x.

$30\% \; of \; x = 12 \Rightarrow 0.30x = 12 \Rightarrow x = 12 \div 0.30 = 40$

36) Choice B is correct

To answer this question, multiply 72 miles per hour to $8 \rightarrow 72 \times 8 = 576$ miles

37) Choice B is correct

Call the missing angle in the top half of the figure y. The sum of the four angles on the top of the figure is equal to $180°$: $x + y + 50 + 60 = 180$

Since y is a vertical angle with the $45°$ angle, then y is also $45°$. Use that to solve for x.

$45 + x + 50 + 60 = 180 \rightarrow 155 + x = 180 \rightarrow x = 25°$

38) Choice D is correct

A. $f(x) = x^2 - 5$ 　　　if 　　　$x = 1 \rightarrow f(1) = (1)^2 - 5 = 1 - 5 = -4 \neq 5$

B. $f(x) = x^2 - 1$ 　　　if 　　　$x = 1 \rightarrow f(1) = (1)^2 - 1 = 1 - 1 = 0 \neq 5$

C. $f(x) = \sqrt{x + 2}$ 　　　if 　　　$x = 1 \rightarrow f(1) = \sqrt{1 + 2} = \sqrt{3} \neq 5$

D. $f(x) = \sqrt{x} + 4$ 　　　if 　　　$x = 1 \rightarrow f(1) = \sqrt{1} + 4 = 5$

39) Choice B is correct

Plug in $\frac{z}{3}$ for z and simplify.

$$x_1 = \frac{8y + \dfrac{r}{r+1}}{\dfrac{z}{3}} = \frac{8y + \dfrac{r}{r+1}}{\dfrac{3 \times 6}{z}} = \frac{8y + \dfrac{r}{r+1}}{3 \times \dfrac{6}{z}} = \frac{1}{3} \times \frac{8y + \dfrac{r}{r+1}}{\dfrac{6}{z}} = \frac{x}{3}$$

40) Choice B is correct

First find the multiples of 8 that fall between 10 and 60: $16, 24, 32, 40, 48, 56$. Since the greatest common factor of 32 and x is 8, x cannot be 32 (otherwise the GCF would be 32, not 8). There are 5 remaining values: $16, 24, 40, 48$ and 56. Number 16 is also not possible (otherwise the GCF would be 16, not 8). Then, there are 4 possible values for x.

41) Choice D is correct

Solve for x: $x^3 + 18 = 130 \rightarrow x^3 = 112$

Let's review the choices.

A. 1 and 2. $1^3 = 1$ and $2^3 = 8$, 112 is not between these two numbers.

B. 2 and 3. $2^3 = 8$ and $3^3 = 27$, 112 is not between these two numbers.

C. 3 and 4. $3^3 = 27$ and $4^3 = 64$, 112 is not between these two numbers.

D. 4 and 5. $4^3 = 64$ and $5^3 = 125$, 112 is between these two numbers.

42) Choice B is correct

Solve for x: $\frac{3x}{25} = \frac{x-1}{5}$, Multiply the second fraction by 5: $\frac{3x}{25} = \frac{5(x-1)}{5 \times 5}$

Tow denominators are equal. Therefore, the numerators must be equal.

$3x = 5x - 5 \rightarrow -2x = -5 \rightarrow \frac{5}{2} = x$

43) Choice B is correct

$(x-2)^3 = 27 \rightarrow x - 2 = 3 \rightarrow x = 5. \rightarrow (x-6)(x-4) = (5-6)(5-4) = (-1)(1) = -1$

44) Choice C is correct

Simplify each choice provided.

A. $20 - (4 \times 10) + (6 \times 30) = 20 - 40 + 180 = 160$

B. $\left(\frac{11}{8} \times 72\right) + \left(\frac{125}{5}\right) = 99 + 25 = 124$

C. $\left(\left(\frac{30}{4} + \frac{13}{2}\right) \times 7\right) - \frac{11}{2} + \frac{110}{4} = \left(\left(\frac{30+26}{4}\right) \times 7\right) - \frac{11}{2} + \frac{55}{2} = \left(\left(\frac{56}{4}\right) \times 7\right) + \frac{55-11}{2} =$

$(14 \times 7) + \frac{44}{2} = 98 + 22 = 120$ (this is the answer)

D. $(2 \times 10) + (50 \times 1.5) + 15 = 20 + 75 + 15 = 110$

45) Choice B is correct

Two triangles ΔBAE and ΔBCD are similar. Then:

$\frac{AE}{CD} = \frac{AB}{BC} \rightarrow \frac{4}{6} = \frac{x}{12} \rightarrow 48 - 4x = 6x \rightarrow 10x = 48 \rightarrow x = 4.8$

46) Choice D is correct

The length of MN is equal to: $3x + 5x = 8x$. Then: $8x = 40 \rightarrow x = \frac{40}{8} = 5$

The length of ON is equal to: $5x = 5 \times 5 = 25\ cm$

47) Choice B is correct

First calculate square of -3: $|-5| + 9 \times 2\frac{1}{3} + 9$

Convert mix number to fraction, then multiply to 9: $|-5| + \frac{63}{3} + 9$

Calculate absolute value and add terms: $5 + 21 + 9 = 35$

48) Choice D is correct

Frist factor the function: $f(x) = x^3 + 8x^2 + 12x = x(x + 2)(x + 6)$, To find the zeros, $f(x)$ should be zero. $f(x) = x(x + 2)(x + 6) = 0$, Therefore, the zeros are: $x = 0$, $(x + 2) = 0 \Rightarrow x = -2$, $(x + 6) = 0 \Rightarrow x = -6$

49) Choice C is correct

Since, E is the midpoint of AB, then the area of all triangles DAE, DEF, CFE and CBE are equal. Let x be the area of one of the triangles, then: $4x = 100 \rightarrow x = 25$

The area of $DEC = 2x = 2(25) = 50$

50) Choice B is correct

These facts are given: F is the midpoint of EH.

EG has a length of x cm. EF has a length of y cm.

Use the first two facts to determine that E has a length of $2y$ centimeters:

$$GH = EH - EG = 2y - x$$

51) Choice C is correct

If $x - a$ is a factor of $g(x)$, then $g(a)$ must equal 0. Based on the table $g(-2) = 0$. Therefore, $x - (-2)$ or $x + 2$ must be a factor of $g(x)$.

52) Choice C is correct

$$\frac{16n^6 - 32n^2 + 8n}{8n} = \frac{16n^6}{8n} - \frac{32n^2}{8n} + \frac{8n}{8n} = 2n^5 - 4n + 1$$

53) Choice B is correct

$$\frac{1\frac{4}{3} + \frac{1}{4}}{2\frac{1}{2} - \frac{17}{8}} = \frac{\frac{7}{3} + \frac{1}{4}}{\frac{5}{2} - \frac{17}{8}} = \frac{\frac{28 + 3}{12}}{\frac{20 - 17}{8}} = \frac{\frac{31}{12}}{\frac{3}{8}} = \frac{31 \times 8}{12 \times 3} = \frac{31 \times 2}{3 \times 3} = \frac{62}{9} \approx 6.88$$

54) Choice D is correct

Check each choice.

A. $\frac{3}{4} > 0.8$ $\frac{3}{4} = 0.75$ and it is less than 0.8. Not true.

B. $10\% = \frac{2}{5}$ $10\% = \frac{1}{10} < \frac{2}{5}$. This is Not True.

C. $3 < \frac{5}{2}$ $\frac{5}{2} = 2.5$. and it is less than 3. Not true.

D. $\frac{5}{6} > 0.8$ $\frac{5}{6} = 0.833$ and it is greater than 0.8. this is True.

55) Choice B is correct

Divide 40 by 4: $\frac{\left(\frac{40(x+1)}{4}\right) - 10}{12} \rightarrow \frac{10(x+1) - 10}{12}$. Distribute 10 through the parentheses $(x + 1)$

$$\frac{10x + 10 - 10}{12} = \frac{10x}{12} = \frac{5}{6}x$$

56) Choice C is correct

40% of 60 equals to: $0.40 \times 60 = 24$. 12% of 600 equals to: $0.12 \times 600 = 72$

40% of 60 is added to 12% of 600: $24 + 72 = 96$

57) Choice A is correct

$$\left(\frac{f}{g}\right)(x) = \frac{f(x)}{g(x)} = \frac{7x - 5}{2x^2 - 4x}$$

58) Choice A is correct

$2x + 4 > 11x - 12.5 - 3.5x \rightarrow$ Combine like terms: $2x + 4 > 7.5x - 12.5 \rightarrow$ Subtract $2x$ from both sides: $4 > 5.5x - 12.5$. Add 12.5 both sides of the inequality. $16.5 > 5.5x$, Divide both sides by $5.5 \rightarrow \frac{16.5}{5.5} > x \rightarrow x < 3$

59) Choice A is correct

$(x + 2)(x + p) = x^2 + (2 + p)x + 2p \rightarrow 2 + p = 6 \rightarrow p = 4 \ and \ r = 2p = 8$

60) Choice B is correct

Simplify the expression. $\sqrt{\frac{x^2}{2} + \frac{x^2}{16}} = \sqrt{\frac{8x^2}{16} + \frac{x^2}{16}} = \sqrt{\frac{9x^2}{16}} = \sqrt{\frac{9}{16}x^2} = \sqrt{\frac{9}{16}} \times \sqrt{x^2} = \frac{3}{4} \times x = \frac{3x}{4}$

... So Much More Online!

Effortless Math Online CLEP College Mathematics Center offers a complete study program, including the following:

- ✓ Step-by-step instructions on how to prepare for the CLEP College Mathematics test

- ✓ Numerous CLEP College Mathematics worksheets to help you measure your math skills

- ✓ Complete list of CLEP College Mathematics formulas

- ✓ Video lessons for CLEP College Mathematics topics

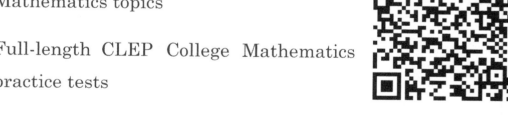

- ✓ Full-length CLEP College Mathematics practice tests

- ✓ And much more...

No Registration Required.

Receive the PDF version of this book or get another FREE book!

Thank you for using our Book!

Do you LOVE this book?

Then, you can get the PDF version of this book or another book absolutely FREE!

Please email us at:

info@EffortlessMath.com

for details.

Author's Final Note

I hope you enjoyed reading this book. You've made it through the book! Great job!

First of all, thank you for purchasing this practice book. I know you could have picked any number of books to help you prepare for your CLEP College Mathematics test, but you picked this book and for that I am extremely grateful.

It took me years to write this workbook for the CLEP College Mathematics because I wanted to prepare a comprehensive CLEP College Mathematics workbook to help test takers make the most effective use of their valuable time while preparing for the test.

After teaching and tutoring math courses for over a decade, I've gathered my personal notes and lessons to develop this practice book. It is my greatest hope that the exercises in this book could help you prepare for your test successfully.

If you have any questions, please contact me at reza@effortlessmath.com and I will be glad to assist. Your feedback will help me to greatly improve the quality of my books in the future and make this book even better. Furthermore, I expect that I have made a few minor errors somewhere in this book. If you think this to be the case, please let me know so I can fix the issue as soon as possible.

If you enjoyed this book and found some benefit in reading this, I'd like to hear from you and hope that you could take a quick minute to post a review on the book's Amazon page. To leave your valuable feedback, please visit: amzn.to/3rZa5ye

Or scan this QR code.

I personally go over every single review, to make sure my books really are reaching out and helping students and test takers. Please help me help CLEP Mathematics test takers, by leaving a review!

I wish you all the best in your future success!

Reza Nazari

Math teacher and author

Made in the USA
Las Vegas, NV
23 January 2022

42192060R00116